ONE DREAM
THE NFL

By Woody Falgoux

Sleeping Bear Press

Sleeping Bear Press
310 North Main Street
P.O. Box 20
Chelsea, MI 48118
www.sleepingbearpress.com

Printed and bound in Canada.

10 9 8 7 6 5 4 3 2 1

Library of Congress Cataloging-in-Publication Data
Falgoux, Woody
 One dream : the NFL / by Woody Falgoux
 p. cm.
ISBN 1-58536-032-5
1. Rookie football players-United States-Biography.
2. New Orleans Saint (Football team) I. Title
GV959 .F35 2001
796.332'092-dc21
[B]
2001020715

THE DREAMERS

Name	Position	College	Hometown
Robert Brannon	Defensive Tackle	Iowa State	Carson, CA
Jamal Brooks	Linebacker	Hampton	Los Angeles, CA
Amp Campbell	Cornerback	Michigan State	Sarasota, FL
D.J. Cooper	Defensive Lineman	Arkansas	Mesquite, TX
Pete Destefano	Safety	California	Morgan Hill, CA
Desmond Gibson	Defensive Tackle	Pittsburgh	Penn Hills, PA
Shayne Graham	Kicker	Virginia Tech	Dublin, VA
Bill LaFleur	Punter	Nebraska	Norfolk, NE
Terrence Miles	Linebacker	Kutztown	Philadelphia, PA
Chase Raynock	Offensive Guard	Montana	Billings, MT

YOU, THE UNDRAFTED ROOKIE

YOUR BOYHOOD DREAM IS HANGING, barely hanging, in the balance. It's all boiled down to 33 days. It's all condensed into five sweaty weeks in a Louisiana kettle. One wrong step, one missed tackle, and the dream evaporates. One blown coverage, one bonehead penalty, and you're cut. You're gone, and no one even notices. They hardly knew you were here. You were just a body. Now, you're only a body bag.

But then there's that chance, a chance measured only in low decimals. There's the opportunity to reach the pinnacle of your sport. It's there if you shock your tribunal, if you perform the way your judges had hoped but never expected.

So you snap on your pads. You step out into the sun and wipe your already beaded brow. You block out the ache in your back and the stiffness in your fingers. You take the field. At first, you're overwhelmed by humans moving as if they were powered by engines, striking as if they were made of steel. It sounds like bulldozers colliding—jet-fueled bulldozers. It feels worse than it sounds. But then somehow, you start to run with them. You buck with them. And later, when the Turk makes his last cut, you're not it. You've made it. You're an NFL football player. And you're a six-figure wage earner possibly on your way to millions.

When the last bit of morning mist burns away from Bayou Lafourche, you head back up the road to New Orleans. Two weeks later, you're floating. It's NFL Sunday. The Superdome lights are shining.

The 'Who Dats' are hooting. You're on the turf. There ain't no mistaking it. Your dream is real.

The NFL dream is the only dream for you and nine other men signed this year by the Saints as undrafted rookies. It's your sole goal, your single focus. Despite your vision, you know that most of the 10 of you, possibly none, will make the team. It's an odd situation for you. You've always been all-everything. Most of your group comes from big-time college programs where you not only started, but starred. Failure has never loomed like it's looming now. If you're cut, you'll not only lose a job, you'll lose a big part of yourself. For the first time in your life, it will be football season, and you won't have a football team. If this happens, you have no idea what you'll do.

At the moment, however, you're not thinking about being cut. You're trying to forget that they said you'd be drafted, but you weren't. You're blocking out the feeling of hearing 254 names called out during the televised draft, and your name not being among them. You know that not being drafted puts you at a supreme disadvantage because the club hasn't put their money and reputation behind you. You don't know exactly what your odds are, but you aren't surprised to learn that last year, only eight percent of all undrafted rookies in training camps made an opening day roster. *Eight percent*. But you can't dwell on this statistic.

You can only set your sights on your quest, an opportunity millions of little boys would love to have but never will. You could care less that you're trying out for one of the historically worst franchises in professional sports, the one with the lowest all-time winning percentage in the NFL. It doesn't matter to you that the Saints have only had five winning seasons in their 33 years of existence. You aren't worried that the "Aints" are the only NFL franchise never to have won a playoff game. It doesn't bother you that your team is said to be cursed for being named after religious figures and for building the Superdome on a cemetery. Your pursuit has nothing to do with the New Orleans Saints, and everything to do with the NFL. It's the league, Baby. And it's almost yours.

THE PRELUDE

CHASE RAYNOCK DOESN'T KNOW IT, but he's staring at a stampede. No one can blame him for being distracted. On this thick August night, the lights are bright and the moon is fat. It's the team's first time in full pads, and the first time any Saint has seen 8,000 people watch a practice. The fans, who have nearly filled this small stadium, are gushing over every flash of black and gold. At the moment, many of them are eyeing Chase. He's about to participate in lineman one-on-ones, which is pure man versus man.

The problem is Chase, an offensive guard, doesn't really understand the degree of man who has lined up a few inches from him. He doesn't know that the saliva is stewing in his opponent's mouth; that the blood is swirling in his brain.

This man, Jared Tomich, already knows everything he needs to know. Part of it is that Chase Raynock is behemoth in size, 6-foot-6, 300-some-odd pounds; part of it is that Chase is greener than the stadium grass. He's an undrafted rookie with boyish blonde hair, a trendy goatee, and eyes as wide and as blue as his native Montana sky. Tomich knows that Chase doesn't have a clue what's coming.

On the other hand, Tomich has been there. He's grunted and grimaced for four years in this league. Before that, he was a snarling defensive lineman at Nebraska. He's been a national champion, an All-American and a starting defensive end in the NFL. But Tomich has more than experience here. He has *motive*. New coaches have come in and given Tomich's job to their top draft pick. They've flat-out handed it to an unlettered bonus-baby-to-be. And now every inch of Tomich wants it back. He's heard all the crap about him being too small at 265 pounds and a little too slow to play d-line in the NFL. He's gonna show all those doubters that they're wrong, and the show starts by blowing up this giant galoot of a rookie.

A coach barks out a snap count and Tomich explodes. He gets under Chase so quickly, Chase can't adjust. Tomich doesn't employ any trickery, any fancy swims or spins. He just bulls Chase, flattens him into mashed potatoes. Within a second, Tomich is on the quarterback, and Chase is one with the worms. Chase's mother couldn't have done any worse.

Afterward, Tomich says Chase was sitting too high in his stance to have any chance at establishing leverage. Tomich admits that he knew exactly what Chase was going to do. "He'll learn to disguise it," says Tomich.

Prying himself off the ground, Chase knows he must learn the tricks and learn them quickly, or he'll be on the first plane back to Billings, Montana. This isn't an exaggeration. The Saints are currently trying to sign two players and bring them into camp. This means two will be cut. More than likely, it is an undrafted rookie who will be sent packing.

About a half an hour later, undrafted rookie D.J. Cooper is not thinking about being released from the team so much as being cut in half by the offensive tackle who is breathing in his direction. He's lined up against the man he calls "The Truth." The Truth is Willie Roaf, who in a few days will be voted by the NFL to its All-Decade team. The Truth is the best player on this field and one of the most dominant blockers on the planet. There's nothing about him that wasn't made to overpower and to outwit. He's built like a big stork, with a barrel chest and skinny legs that give him both speed and agility. His genes are impeccable. He is the child of a dentist and an Arkansas judge. Yes, The Truth fits him in every way.

Coop is trying to decide what do with The Truth. Coop's pass rush skills are rooted in his adolescent kickboxing—three knockouts, two technical knockouts, no losses—but he can't kickbox an intelligent, quick-footed wall of steel. While he can't box him, he can fox him. He might not have a professional pedigree, but he's got plenty of Texas crunk. He was so crunked up this morning he vomited. But he can think clearly now. He knows he must do what no rook would try against The Truth the first time he's ever faced him in full pads.

Coop is trying to get into The Truth's mind. He believes The Truth is thinking this Cooper cat is undrafted, which means his forty time is too slow, and his bench press too low, which should mean he can't whoop me physically. Coop knows The Truth has watched him get into two fights in one day of spring minicamp, both with Kyle Turley, The Truth's nasty linemate. In one of these bouts, Coop did some kind of running kick at Turley. So the rookie's got fire and crazy moves. So, Coop figures, his opponent's focus is the flash, not the force.

When the coach counts it out, Coop detonates. It's all raw, blunt thrust, and The Truth isn't ready for it. He rocks in reverse. He loses his footing. He's on his back. Coop is so amazed he stares downward for a split-second before running toward the quarterback. He looks around. He hopes they're paying attention.

Of course, they're paying attention. They always are. They see it first in person. They see it again on film. Three video cameras make sure of that. Every move is ripe for analysis and overanalysis, praise or ridicule. If you're Coop and you bull, or if you're Chase and you get bulled, they will all watch you and watch you and watch you.

Watching, however, is not so much what one man is doing as he is basking. Saints' owner Tom Benson is strolling down the sidelines, waving at the whooping Who Dats in each grandstand, bathing in their adoration. They are standing on their feet, clapping. To them, the old man is Santa Claus. He has given them back their boys. For the first time in 12 years, the 'Saints are training in Louisiana. For the first time in 25 years, they are camping in the state's bayou country.

There are many firsts here, and Benson is ultimately responsible for all of them. He's the one who came into work one day last year and allegedly rolled every head in the building. He's the one who then hired the new general manager, who signed up the new coach, who brought over the new assistants, who are coaching all these new players. It's all so new, new, new.

/ ONE /

IF WE REBUILD IT

No one could honestly believe the NFL would come back here. Here is Thibodaux, the site of one of the most disastrous camps in league history. Camp Thibodaux 1975 was biblically catastrophic. It was Old Testament stuff, sending plagues only Moses could prophesy. There were the monsoons, the mosquitoes, the bus rides, the bug zappers, the scalding heat, and the coach who forgot to put lamb's blood on his dorm room door. There was also plenty of darkness, the kind of dim light that comes when you're on your way to a ninth straight losing season.

But in the summer of '75, it had seemed like a good idea. Take the boys out of their Vero Beach, Florida training camp country club and bring them back to the bayou. Send them to Thibodaux, a charming little Cajun town an hour's drive from the city with a quaint little college, Nicholls State University. Send them to the land of live oaks and cypress, Spanish moss and azaleas, Acadian cottages and sugarcane plantations, all lined up along Bayou Lafourche. Sure, they wouldn't exactly be staying at Rienzi Plantation, but roughing it would be good for 'em. Something needed to reverse eight straight years of winning no more than five games a season.

From the moment the Saints hit campus that year, the mosquitoes never gave them a chance. They swarmed from the adjacent sugarcane fields and crossed the road to the practice area. And no one was prepared. It didn't matter that the university sprayed the practice fields with mosquito dope and hung bug zappers along the sidelines. It didn't matter that the players were issued cans of repellent. The skeets sucked the lifeblood out of the lineman and the juice from the wide receivers.

What might have been worse were the buzzing zappers. Hung all around the pitch, they were murdering mosquitoes so quickly that the noise was deafening. The zapping got so loud at times the offense couldn't hear quarterback Archie Manning call plays in the huddle.

The Saints might have put up with the mosquitoes had they been able to stand the deluge. It was a nonstop, day-after-day downpour. It turned the fields into marshlands, forcing the Saints to retreat. They started busing the players into the city to practice on the artificial turf at Tulane Stadium. In between two-a-day practices, the road warriors would crash on sheetless mattresses in a Tulane dorm. After the second session, they'd bus back into bayou country to sleep at Nicholls State. With one week of camp to go, the Saints called it quits and returned to New Orleans.

Six games into that cursed season, head coach John North was beheaded, and the Saints finished 2-12.

Before the 1976 season, when it came time to decide on a training camp, it didn't take Moses to know that the Saints would avoid a place where pestilence might run rampant again. They went back to their Florida resort and as the years passed, to other places that weren't called Thibodaux.

Then, as the millennium turned, the Saints began to think about moving their training camp from LaCrosse, Wisconsin, where it had been for the previous 12 years. They talked about leaving the cool dells and dairy farms of the northern hinterlands and returning to the subtropics. At first, it didn't seem plausible, considering that their last camp in the region, in Hammond, Louisiana, resulted in an onslaught of dehydration cases.

Then again, looking at the bottom line, the *real* bottom line, it made sense. Tickets sales were on the decline, and there were more potential purchasers in the Gulf South than there were in the Great Lakes. So the cities lined up and made their bids. The Saints were wooed by Hammond and Lafayette and Mobile, Alabama. Then, out of nowhere came Thibodaux, calling the Saints to come back to the very spot where Jim Bowie once lived, the very soil on which he fought Chitimachans with his famous knife.

The folks at Nicholls figured there was nothing wrong with a phone call. The call led to a visit. The Saints sent their dignitaries, and lo and behold, the dignitaries wanted to negotiate. During the course of the negotiations, many demands were made. Nicholls had subpar I-AA facilities that needed to be upgraded. The renovations would take a lot more money than the university had in its kitty. But the Powers That Be decided that they would find the funds from somewhere. This was the *NFL* that was at stake. This was the way for college officials, politicians, and average Joe Boudreauxs to participate in the NFL, to touch it, to taste it, to imbibe its economic impact.

So the dealmakers went to work, led by Thibodaux Mayor Charles Caillouet. Within a few days, Caillouet and company secured pledges of $100,000 from the City of Thibodaux, $100,000 from the State of Louisiana, $50,000 from Lafourche Parish, and $50,000 from nearby Terrebonne Parish.

But what about the mosquitoes? the Saints asked. Thibodaux answered. Ironically, Thibodaux already had a mosquito abatement program in the works. Its citizens didn't enjoy coexisting with the little pests any more than did an NFL football player. So the city put its already-planned $85,000 program on the fast track, and shortly thereafter, a mosquito-abating airplane began to bomb the fields weekly with insecticide.

But what about the monsoons? the Saints asked. Thibodaux answered by seeking help from its neighbors in Terrebonne Parish. Terrebonne volunteered its civic center for rainy days and then temporarily floored the building with 60 by 60 yards of borrowed Superdome turf.

And just like that, the Saints were coming. It didn't matter that the progressive-minded members of the Lafourche Parish Council decided to renege on their president's promise and vote down his $50,000 pledge. It didn't even matter that Councilman Charles Banta of Chackbay put a sign on a telephone pole near his house that read, "I *Will Not* Give The Saints Your Tax Money" (None of the money would actually go to the Saints. It all went toward improving the university infrastructure.)

The goal of all of these improvements was increased comfort, better hygiene, and most importantly, injury prevention. Increased comfort meant buying full-sized beds and individual-line telephones for the dorm rooms. It also meant repainting, relighting and recarpeting every square centimeter of the locker room, recovering the training tables, reconfiguring the lockers, adding extra hooks, sanding the bathroom floors, polishing the plumbing fixtures, and installing extra shelves above the sinks.

Better hygiene meant adding soap dispensers to the showers so the players wouldn't have to share bar soap. "I don't know about you," said Camp Coordinator Mike Davis. "But after you finish showering, I don't want to borrow your soap."

In the end, the place became more than just a sterile, sparkling, NFL-quality locker room. It became the halls of Shambala.

Then there was the matter of injury-proofing the campus. NFL coaches are just plain petrified of injuries, and, economically speaking, they should be. In the NFL, players aren't just athletes, they're millionaires. The fewer millionaires on the field, the fewer entries in the win column and the more likely the head coach is to lose his job and his million-dollar salary. So a coach, especially a rookie head coach like the Saints' Jim Haslett, will go to seemingly ridiculous lengths to prevent injuries.

In Thibodaux 2000, this meant Haslett didn't want his players to walk or ride their bikes on the shell road that led back to the locker facility. To him, the shell and gravel mix was potentially lethal. It could trip, scrape, hyper-extend, sever, separate, tear. Consequently, a paved sidewalk was installed alongside the dangerous shell road. The players could now walk on safe, level ground.

In Haslett's opinion, the practice fields were far from safe and level. By NFL standards, they were as dangerous as a minefield. Their sizes, one 100-yard pitch and two 70-yarders, were the only things that were remotely acceptable. Despite being located in green, rockless country, the fields were hard as granite and full of holes. The grass was composed of 95% weeds, which included swarms of prickly cockleburs.

Enter Terry Ashburn, the Saints' turf expert. As soon as Ashburn hit campus, he huddled the Nicholls grounds crew together, and the workers attacked, slicing and dicing the fields. Next, they dumped golf course grade sand into the slivers, not stopping until they'd poured in 160 tons of it, turning the old concrete-like surfaces into soft fairways, shaping them into symmetrical turtlebacks. Along the way, the crew doused the fields with fertilizer, herbicides, fungicides and ant poison, filled the holes with fresh sod, and revamped the antiquated drainage by installing a piping system.

All along, the crew watered and watered and watered. It had been an unusually dry spring, and the crew compensated for it by running hoses from all over campus to drench what had been transformed into an almost pure patch of Bermuda. In fact, on the evening before camp began, two trucks from the Thibodaux Volunteer Fire Department sent their hoses up ladders 100 feet into the air and shot geysers over the field at the rate of one thousand gallons per minute, leaving big puddles everywhere. For the first day of practice, the fields would have to be as cottony as possible.

$\sim$

Now, as the fire trucks pull away, the time shifts to the present. On this eve of camp, the fields glimmer a lush gold green in the fading light. They seem to undulate like waves. They flow all the way to the new silver fence, which stands around the perimeter. The fence, along with a row of live oak trees, is the only thing that breaks the fields' connection to the neighboring rows of sugarcane.

With the tall stalks of cane swaying and the new grass growing, with the white yard lines gleaming and the aluminum bleachers beaming, the setting reminds one of a certain movie. But instead of Shoeless Joe Jackson and ancient baseball players coming out of the corn, old pro football players are emerging from the cane. There's Willie Brown and Willie Wood. There's Larry Little and Emlen Tunnel, Jim Langer and Night Train Lane. All are enshrined in the Pro Football Hall of Fame, and all got their start as undrafted rookies.

/ TWO /

A FESTIVAL CALLED TRAINING CAMP

SATURDAY, JULY 15, 2000, 8:30 A.M.

Undrafted rookie punter Bill LaFleur has just left the air-conditioned locker room, and rivers of sweat are already running down his face. The sun is cooking his skin, turning it pinker by the second. But as big as this blazing yellow orb is, it's not as large as the competition. To earn a spot on the roster, Bill must justify that he's good enough for the Saints to throw away six hundred grand. He's got to prove that it's worth it for the team to blow off the high six-figure bonus they paid to a veteran punter to lure him from the Dallas Cowboys. The proof process starts now in warm-ups, one hour before practice begins.

After a half hour, Bill's uniform is as soaked as it would be if he'd been cutting cane all day while wearing a gorilla suit. He has to dry his hands before picking up a ball for another drop and boot. About this time, his teammates start to make their way down the chute. The first group heads immediately for the shade of a live oak tree. They better enjoy it. By tomorrow, standing in the shade will be forbidden.

Under the oak, the players pause and take in the setting, hardly believing that they're looking at a training camp. In their general manager's words, it looks more like "Disneyland." His description has a little something to do with the 3,000 fans that have piled into the bleachers and lined the fence, many pausing periodically to wipe the sweat that has dripped from their foreheads into their sunglasses. It has a lot to do with the celebration city that is perched between the practice fields and John

L. Guidry Stadium. It's a festival of tents. There're enough of them to encamp a small Middle Eastern army. There are game tents, food tents, and air-conditioned, fully catered corporate tents. There are tents rented by businesses to market everything from acupuncture to financial advice to laser vision correction. Even the Armed Forces have a tent, proving Uncle Sam never misses an opportunity.

In addition to all the tent warfare and welfare, there's music. Scheduled to perform almost every day of camp are an assortment of local bands, who will jam from a nice-sized bandstand. There's also a first class port-a-let trailer, full of cool air and clean toilets. For the kids, there's "Junior Training Camp." It's where the youngsters can test their skills by throwing footballs through tires, hitting tackling dummies and traversing through obstacle courses.

So the children will play, and adults will eat jambalaya and drink beer. And next to all this revelry, warmth and good feeling, gigantic men will be beating the hell out of each other. Just as a little girl guesses the right number and wins a pink bear, a safety will hit a wide receiver so hard that his vertebrae will vibrate. At the same time a boy makes a bottle stand up with a rope and wins a plastic football, a lineman will punch another lineman in the solar plexus. When practice ends, and the band starts playing, the fans will whoop and dance, and the football players will stagger off the field, panting, aching, barely escaping dehydration.

~

At 9:30 a.m. sharp, an air horn blows, and there is a chorus of shouts. "Let's go! Let's go! Let's go!" The team charges onto the middle of the field and comes together in a huddle. They are high-fiving, shoulder-slapping, clapping. The fans are exploding. Their roar raises and dies. The players turn toward them and wave for more cheer. They get it. The fans lift their voices to new levels.

The day is so new. The sun is so bright. The field is as plush and green and as beautiful as it will ever be. It is almost virgin. There are no cleat rips or divots. There are barely any footprints. It will never again be this fresh, this innocent. Nothing here will. They're all a team. Each is a part. For some of them, it may never get any better than this.

~

For Carlos Posey, it never even got this good. Somehow, he never made it here.

Going into the April 2000 draft, Posey was considered a draftable player, a probable late round pick. The former Missouri Tiger was known as a cornerback with the speed of a collegiate sprinter, but with raw coverage skills. While he was passed over in the draft, Posey was happy to sign a free agent contract with the Saints. Having been raised just up I-10 in Baton Rouge, Posey was fulfilling a childhood fantasy.

Then, at the first minicamp, he severely sprained his right ankle and never made it back to a spring practice. There were 20-plus practices this spring, most of them called "coaching sessions," which were basically practices without full pads. Despite missing all of this crucial instructional time, Posey was gearing up for training camp, hoping his ankle would be good to go when the horn sounded.

Then four days ago, the phone rang at Posey's Baton Rouge residence. It was a young man named—"something Neil, O'Neil." The man told Posey that he was calling on behalf of Saints' General Manager Randy Mueller. Posey's ears perked up. The voice told him he'd been released from the team. Posey got quiet. He knew it was a cutthroat business, but he didn't know that his own throat was about to be slashed.

"It hurt me, you know," he said a day later, still sounding a bit confused. "I just got to deal with it. I can't let it bring me down."

But it's difficult to stay up in a situation like his. He knows that no team is likely to sign an undrafted player who is still recovering from an injury, someone without any preseason game film.

"They didn't really see what I had," said Posey. He never fathomed not making it to the first day of camp. "I thought they would give me at least a shot."

The Saints never gave him a shot because they had to trim the roster to 87 for the start of training camp. To get there, they had to release three players. As to why one of those players was Posey and not someone else, Randy Mueller was frank. "We never saw him," said Mueller. "It comes down to numbers, and someone has to go. And sometimes the easiest guy to go is the guy you've never seen before. It's not really fair. It's just the way it is."

It's also just the way it is that Posey was cut by someone he never even met. The messenger was Grant Neil, a player personnel assistant whose spectacles and slicked back hair make him look like someone working for corporate America.

Neil's message was one that he had no previous experience in delivering, and he was nervous as he dialed Carlos Posey's number. "It's tough," he said. "I mean, you know, you're telling a guy, basically, he's fired. It's hard. It's an uncomfortable call to make."

Neil doesn't know if he'll be designated as the training camp "Turk," the Saints' staffer who tells the players face-to-face that they've been released. "Randy's the boss of this team, and if Randy asked me to do something, whether I like it or not, I'm going to do it, and I'm going to do it professionally, and try to be as understanding as possible."

The undrafted rookies in camp certainly understand that there will be a Turk, and that if they don't play well, beginning now, Day 1, Practice 1, the Turk will find them.

~

Perhaps it's the fear of the Turk, perhaps it's his ferociously competitive spirit that makes undrafted rookie safety Pete Destefano want to win at every single thing he does. At present, the northern Californian is trying to beat his mates at a karoka drill. This is a warm-up exercise that most players perform mindlessly. It certainly isn't a competition to them. But it's not that way with Pete. Pete gives his all every time, whether he's terrorizing blocking sleds or blazing through wind sprints. While, a half hour ago, the others walked or jogged onto the field, Pete ran. While veteran backup quarterback Billy Joe Tolliver strolled down the chute and inserted a dip into his cheek and gum, Pete kept his helmet on, his fists clinched, and his face determined. Really, it's his face that tells it. It's not the 6-2, 217, 3% body fat physique with the traps that taper like ramps from his midneck. It's the face, chiseled and square, sitting beneath close-cropped hair, holding a pair of intense green eyes. The face looks like it belongs in an old leather helmet. It makes him look that tough, throwback tough.

Pete and the rest of the players must be especially resilient this morning because the elements aren't easing up on them. Although Pete will later say, "I thought it was going to be hotter, actually," this is just Pete's pride talking. The fact is it's simply molten out here. The temperature is 98°, the heat index is at 104°, but numbers hardly tell the tale. The real story is that south Louisiana is a low-lying, wet place with air that stays liquid and still. Thibodaux itself sits on ground that is barely above sea level. The town is surrounded by swampland, and below that marshland, and below that the Gulf of Mexico. In the late summer, the air never dries and rarely moves.

~

Midway through practice, the asphyxiating atmosphere is starting to mess with undrafted rookie defensive tackle Robert Brannon. He is breathing hard and struggling. In a team drill, he bumps heads with a fellow defensive lineman and starts to feel dizzy. He crashes to the ground. Someone yells, "Trainer!" and the sports medicine people run toward the fallen giant with the big baby face. Robert stays conscious, but remains woozy as the trainers heave him into a cart and ride him to the locker room.

After practice, Robert swears the injury, a mild concussion, had nothing to do with the heat. "He just hit my head," he says, "and I don't know what happened after that."

But Robert's coaches seem to believe that his problems involved more than just bumping helmets. Haslett says that Robert must get in better shape if he wants to make the football team. Robert's defensive line coach, Sam Clancy, is even more blunt. "Any injury to a free agent rookie is not good for him," says Clancy. "So he'll have to get back on the field pretty soon, really, if he wants an opportunity to make the ball club. And that's just the reality of football up here."

Notwithstanding Robert's injury, Clancy isn't too happy with his young lineman, who, at 22, is the youngest player here. Even before Robert's arrival, he set the wrong tone. First, he reported to camp late, and second, he came in 18 pounds overweight. Now, with other defensive lineman nursing injuries and one not yet in camp, Robert is missing out on a prime opportunity.

For Robert's fellow undrafted rookies, a new opportunity beckons. At tonight's practice, the team will dress for the first time in full pads. Finally, they will put on a suit of armor and go into battle.

Throughout the spring practices, the coaches have been asked if they could tell a player's true ability in shorts and shells. And all of them give an answer similar to offensive line coach Jack Henry's. "You can't tell," says Henry. "I mean the game's not to be played in your underwear. It's to be played in pads. And we'll start finding out some of that tonight."

/ THREE /

ALL AMPED UP

Saturday, July 15, 2000, 7:15 p.m.

A big shadow is moving across Guidry Stadium, cloaking the field with anticipation. The sky is bleeding orange, and the atmosphere is oozing electricity. Eight thousand fans are already stirring in their seats. Many of them are already howling at the full moon. It feels like a game, but it's only a practice.

As for the undrafted rookies, they compare it to the Friday night lights of high school football, but they know they're light-years from there. They knew it in April as soon as they hit the Saints' headquarters in Metairie. At the time, each was given a quick sign that he wasn't in college anymore. It was that little something that told them, "This is the NFL."

Bill LaFleur knew it as soon as he turned off Airline Highway. "I looked out there, and I saw those neon yellow kind of goalposts," says Bill. "And you just get that feeling in your stomach. This is what it's about. This is what I dreamed about."

Pete Destefano saw the NFL in a parking lot full of Jags, Hummers, and other opulent automobiles. "People have different drives, what drives them. For me, I want to have the money. I'm not necessarily materialistic. I like to work hard. For me, seeing every single player have those cars, going up and seeing the Lexuses, the sport utility vehicles, the Mercedes, I went, 'Wow,' you know. For me, I don't know, you've arrived when you get a car."

For Chase Raynock and defensive tackle Desmond Gibson, it was a sense of being starstruck. "Willie Roaf," remembers Chase. "That's really Willie Roaf, and you're sitting in the same room with him, doing the same meetings, you know."

D.J. Cooper wasn't so much starstruck as he was "size-struck." "The first person I seen when I first got there was (Willie) Whitehead, and he was on crutches," says Coop. "And that's a big yoked dude! I ain't never seen no, you know, them people like that are rare. Hey, that's a big ol' dude on crutches, man."

Linebacker Terrence Miles couldn't get over how organized everything was in the facility. He couldn't believe his equipment was already in his locker. Fellow linebacker Jamal Brooks had a similar experience. After finishing his workout and throwing his clothes in the laundry hamper, he went off to watch film. When he got back, his clothes were already washed. Later that day, a trainer showed him all the snacks and supplements at his disposal. "It was an *array* of stuff," says Jamal. "I was like you know back in college, you'd be happy (because) we just got to take creatine my senior year. I was like they (the Saints) got powders for muscle mass, for rip, for energy. They got so much stuff to take, bananas, fruits, a thing of Gatorade, a lot of materialistic little plush stuff."

It was the plush stuff that also caught placekicker Shayne Graham's eye when he got his first tryout in the spring with the Cleveland Browns. He remembers walking into the locker room. "It was like a barbershop. Every sink had, you know, shaving cream and everything you needed." After his first morning in Saints' gear, Shayne says, "You never turn a corner or do anything where there isn't someone offering you a Gatorade or a water or any convenience that you normally wouldn't have."

Across the board, the undrafted rookies were blown away by the speed of the professional game, which was evident in the first minicamp. Robert Brannon still scratches his head over it. "I never went shells, without no pads on, full go. I never went like that. It was like, 'Dang man, they going like this, this early?' People could get hurt."

Given defensive back Amp Campbell's medical history, getting hurt should have been a consideration. Anyone who has heard his skull being grinded and bored would probably be thinking about the prospect of injury. But he wasn't. What Amp remembers about the first day of minicamp was the uniform. "Once I put that helmet on, you know, it just gave me the jitters."

Tonight, as Amp runs out to participate in a seven-on-seven drill, he eases into the now familiar Saints' helmet, and although it's his first time in a full pads as a pro, the dress code isn't any different than in college. What is different and a little unsettling to him is that he's just been moved to a new position, safety. Safety is not as safe and comfortable to him as cornerback, where Amp was an All-American last year at Michigan State.

Corner is one of the trickiest positions in the game, but Amp has always called it home. In college, Amp quickly developed a reputation for shutting down the Big Ten's best receivers. A quiet person by nature, Amp let his performance talk for him as he racked up 14 pass breakups as a sophomore, 15 as a junior, and a nation-leading 24 breakups as a senior.

But now, things out on the field look all broken up. He's not nosed up to a Saints' receiver near the line of scrimmage, where he usually is. He's a long way from there, way back in the foreign deep half. He doesn't understand how this happened. In the first minicamp, they put him at safety right away, but after seeing his discomfort with the position, they shifted him to corner and watched him turn it on. He was suddenly smooth, natural. "He's got real good football instincts," says Saints' defensive backs coach Rick Venturi. "I mean he understands the game. I don't know if it's so much mental, but instinctively, he instinctively knows what to do."

But back there now at safety, it doesn't feel as instinctive. He looks over and sees another rookie, a sixth-round draft pick, Michael Hawthorne, occupying his cornerback position. Hawthorne is crouching his tall, skinny frame into a stance that used to be Amp's.

Amp would never publicly verbalize this, but he doesn't get it. He's known Hawthorne for a long time. The two of them first teamed up in a Pop Warner league back in Sarasota, Florida. They both played for the Mohawks, both ran around the field to the sound of dirt bikes revving and purring on a nearby track. Later, they both starred at separate Sarasota high schools, then both played corner at separate Big Ten schools, with Hawthorne attending Purdue. At the 2000

Gridiron Classic All-Star game, they started at opposite corners for the Team Florida squad. Now together again at Saints' camp as room-mates, Amp has to wonder why they're moving him, and not Hawthorne.

As for Hawthorne, he doesn't believe being drafted gives him an edge. He says through his gold-capped teeth in a very confident tone, "If I wasn't drafted, hey, I'd still come and out and do what Michael Hawthorne does best. I'll bring my six-three, 200 pound, 4.3-running self to practice."

Maybe it's the speed, or the lack thereof, that prompted Amp's move. Hawthorne is faster than Amp, at least in a footrace. But he's not the cover man that Amp is. He didn't come close to performing at Amp's level in college.

Amp, though, won't talk about any of that. He's not going to knock Hawthorne or anyone else. He isn't going to make any excuses. And if he wanted to, he could certainly make them. Anyone who breaks his neck is entitled to an excuse or two.

~

Amp heard the words so many times. "You're not gonna play again. You're not gonna play again." He didn't turn his ear to them. He used them as motivation. He refused to forget what happened that Thursday night in September 1998, on the wet astroturf in Eugene, Oregon. He wanted to remember it. He had to know exactly what he was going to overcome.

On that night, in the first quarter, the Oregon Duck offense was perched near the goal line. The ball snapped, and the fullback came barreling toward the Michigan State defense and the end zone. Amp met him at the half-inch line, lowered his head and slipped. His head struck his opponent's thigh. The impact jarred his neck. Amp laid down flat, rolled over and took off his helmet. He thought it was only a stinger. Seconds later, medical people were asking him all these questions. As he walked with them to the sideline, he noticed he couldn't see the scoreboard. He was dizzy and getting dizzier. When he made it to the bench, he didn't want to sit. He wanted to lay, and that's what he did all the way to the hospital.

At first, Amp figured it couldn't be any worse than a separated shoulder. All he thought about was how he'd let down a friend from Sarasota who had driven from nearby Oregon State to watch the game. He couldn't believe it when the surgeon explained to him that his neck was broken enough to paralyze most people, and that he was lucky that he was in such great shape, or he, too, would have been paralyzed. While the doctor calmly explained how "simple" the procedure was, there seemed to be nothing simple about removing a bone from your hip, then cutting your throat to create an entry point to place the hipbone between your C6 and C7 vertebra and fusing them all together.

Amp remembers the nurses coming in every five minutes to test for feeling in his fingers and toes. At some point, he fell asleep, and at some point, he woke up. In between was the surgery, the "easy" part. Nothing would anesthetize him for the remainder of the recovery, including the next step, which was the fitting of a halo, which would be screwed into his skull to set in place the fused vertebra.

"Having a needle being stuck in your skull, and then you're hearing stuff crunching," says Amp. "And then the doctor tell me he's going to put screws into your head. You just hear it. You feeling it twisting tight and pulling on your neck."

He was on his back strapped to a bed, with 70 pounds of weight pulling against the halo. When they rolled him by a mirror, he couldn't believe it was him. For two days after the surgery, he was too sore to talk, or to swallow. "When I was in the hospital bed, I couldn't get up and use the phone. I couldn't get out of bed and go to the bathroom. I couldn't get up and go to McDonald's."

It humbled him. "I thought I was invincible," he says. It also made him realize he would have to rely on others for a while. His parents flew out there the day after the accident. They stayed with him for the next three days in the hospital. During that time, many people told him to go home, sit out the remainder of the semester and just chill. He wouldn't hear of it. "The things that were going through my head with them telling me I'm not going to be able to play football any more, I had to get this degree." He said he didn't want to mope all day in Sarasota so he returned to East Lansing, and while his mother, Pearl, had to go back to work, his father, Johnnie, who is disabled with a hip-related condition, stayed with him in Michigan.

As the halo came off before Amp left the hospital, a special brace came on. It stretched from his earlobes all the way to his waist. It was so cumbersome he couldn't fit in a classroom chair. So he stood, for the entire class, for class after class, all semester and for four months altogether. At home, his father was his "backbone." Every day, Johnnie Campbell bathed his son, clothed him, tied his shoes.

The inspiration for Amp to plow ahead was coming from many directions, from his father, from his high school sweetheart, Denise Springer, from his then two-year-old daughter, Kiera, from his friends and coaches and from people he'd never even met. There was a get-well letter that really struck him. It was written by a woman from Grand Rapids who had been battling cancer for two years. "She told me, 'Never quit,' and she said she never asked God why this happened to her. And she said, 'Don't ask God why this happened to you.' And I never did."

Amp finished the semester, returned for another one and graduated that summer. He earned a telecommunications degree, an honor that once looked doubtful when he was declared academically ineligible for his redshirt freshman year. With the diploma under his arm, football was next. While there may have been tears and doubt in the early days, he was now all go. He had to do this for Kiera, for others who had received devastating injuries, and for himself, for his utter love of the game.

When two-a-days started at Michigan State in August of 1999, he hit the field. His only thought about the injury was the lesson he learned about not leading with his head. In the very first game of the season, against none other than Oregon, he would put the injury emphatically behind him. The Ducks may have damn near paralyzed him, but that day, he would beat them. He, personally, would be the difference between his Spartans winning or losing that game. In the fourth quarter, he scooped a fumble and returned it 85 yards for the game-winning touchdown.

His mere presence at practice every day inspired his team and his head coach, Nick Saban, who is now the coach at LSU. After Saban announced to the Michigan State team in December of 1999 that he was leaving to take the job at LSU, he approached Amp and asked him to come to his office. Once they were behind closed doors, the usually

calm, emotionless Saban had a hard time getting out his words. He
started to choke up, and he and Amp both just broke down. It is still difficult for Saban to talk at length about Amp without getting emotional.

It is no longer emotional for Amp to just get out of bed in the
morning, but he hasn't forgotten his blessings. Every time he takes the
field, he recites a self-written prayer. It begins, "I thank God for this
day." So if the day means playing safety for the Saints, that's fine with
him. It's okay because it will be a long camp, with ample time to watch
extra film, to memorize the encyclopedic playbook and to get enough
reps to master the new position. Playing safety is an opportunity, and
every opportunity is a gift.

$\sim$

Later in practice, a gift is being tipped into the air for Jamal
Brooks, who snatches it. He makes the interception and runs 10 yards
for the score. He's thankful he saw it, grabbed it, made the play. *Make
plays*—this is what is said over and over to the undrafted. Make a play
and stay. Make a mistake, and you're cake. Much of playmaking, Jamal
knows, depends on fortuity, fate, God's will. So when the ball's in the
air, and he, as a linebacker, has a rare chance to make a pick, he knows
he better make it.

After practice, Jamal is carrying three of the veteran linebackers'
shoulder pads. It's "rookie stuff," mild hazing by the "older heads."
Jamal isn't complaining. "I'd rather carry pads after practice in the
NFL than be at home in the A/C sipping on lemonade," he says. He's
grateful for tonight's cooler temperatures and absolutely exuberant
about playing football after not getting an opportunity in 1999, when
no one drafted him or offered him a free agent contract coming out of
college.

Now, though, he knows that he must learn fast. A point he makes
often is, "I gotta slow the game down." It's so thick and so quick in
there at linebacker, it's easy to miss your gap, miss the coverage, miss
the tackle by barely a hair or think your way into playing too tentatively.
"They say, A, you 'posed to know what you 'posed to know, B, know
how to do it, and C, be aggressive." He says about wearing full pads,
"Man, I can concentrate more because I know it's 'Get there, boom.

Get there.' But I still gotta learn how to *slow* down a little bit. Don't overplay because we're in pads."

It's odd that they're in full gear, yet the action really isn't full throttle. Only the blocking is all out. There is no tackling, only a chest-to-chest thump. Tackling increases the risk of injury, which Coach Haslett is trying so earnestly to avoid. But Jamal claims Haslett's rule doesn't limit him. "If you can come up in somebody's face and thud 'em, you basically should be able to tackle 'em." Still, tackling is the root of defensive football, and one has to wonder how an undrafted rookie defender can prove himself without being able to finish the play, without being able to wrap up and drag the ballcarrier to the ground.

~

At 9:30 p.m., practice concludes but not the festivities. The fans are treated to fireworks, with the final boom punctuated by the lighting of an oversized, freestanding *fleur-de-lis* in the end zone.

One man in the crowd watches the Saints' symbol illuminate and has to smile. He has seen himself come full circle with the NFL. First, he reached out to the league, and now it has literally come back to him, with a training camp landing 20 miles from his home. As a kid growing up just down the bayou in Mathews, Mike Detillier dreamed of playing in the NFL one day. But he realized, while playing high school football, that he would never be good enough to reach that level. Nevertheless, the 40-year-old's fascination with the NFL never left him.

Somehow, Detillier has taken his youthful fantasy and turned it into a nice living. He is an "NFL analyst," analyzing every facet of the league. He has no off-season and hasn't held another occupation since he left a welding supply sales job in 1989. His residence on Adams Street in Mathews may appear to be just another neat, modest house on the lane. But inside, his home office is NFL command central. Its walls are full of autographed pictures of pro football legends. Its bookshelves are lined with a football library. His primary tools are a computer, a television, a telephone, and a videotape player. Several times a week, he goes live from the lane on several regional radio call-in shows. Right from his office, he films a segment for a weekly national cable television show, "All-Star Football," on Prime Sports Network. He also writes a local newspaper column and answers questions on a Saints-related web site. Additionally, he does freelance scouting work for NFL Europe and the XFL.

While Detillier's always game to talk anything NFL, his primary focus is the draft. He has been self-publishing the *M & D Draft Report* since 1986. In it, he evaluates all of the draftable players coming out of college for the upcoming spring draft. He rates them, gives their strengths, their weaknesses. His preparation for his report is ongoing. He reviews 700-800 videos per year, each tape of a different college player. Some are sent to him; others he requests. And every weekend, he's either watching prospects play in person, or he's glued to his television set, watching games that take place from coast to coast, filling his notepad with ink. In a year's time, he'll make thousands of phone calls, to players' coaches, to coaches who have coached against a particular player. He gets the scoop from any source he can.

"I'm friends with a lot of scouts in this league," says Detillier in a Cajun accent that's hardly affected by all his radio days. "We kind of intertwine our information. 'Hey, who you hear's looking pretty good? Who you hear's not?' And so there's a lot of crisscrossing information that goes on. So it's a funny little network of how it's done."

Even though Detillier tries to gather as much information and as many opinions as he can, he himself must write his conclusion about a player. "You have to make the decision how well he'll adjust from college to the professional. That, no one can tell you. You got to make that particular decision yourself."

At this point, some decisions need to be made about the Saints' 10 undrafted rookies. After tonight's practice, we learn that the team will have to cut someone tomorrow. That someone could be one of the 10 rookie free agents. Detillier has been following them since college. He has given me his opinions about who has the best chances of being one of the 53 players chosen for the final roster or the five additional players selected to the practice squad. Opinions have also come from the Saints' beat writers, who have been covering the team since the first minicamp. I, the author, have to enter myself into this picture. I have to consider what Detillier has told me, what the writers have written, what the coaches have said, what I saw at the last minicamp, and what I saw today.

The consensus is anywhere from one to three of the undrafted will make this team, either on the roster or the practice squad. My best guess is that come opening day, September 3, 2000, when the Saints take on the Detroit Lions, at least one of these three young men will still be in Saintstown: Amp Campbell, D.J. Cooper, and/or Pete Destefano.

But that's merely a prediction. It's not the certainty of what's coming. Tomorrow morning, the sun will certainly rise, and the Turk will definitely strike.

/ FOUR /

ENTER IGOR, THE TURK

SUNDAY, JULY 16, 2000, 6:45 A.M.

All I can do is wait. I don't know how or when or who they're going to cut. So I arrive early. I perch in the Saints media relations' office in Guidry Stadium like I'm sitting on a deer stand. When, after a half hour, the Saints media relations' chief tells me whom he thinks they're going to cut, my heart skips. I don't believe him. So I sit there in denial, get up and leave, come back, leave again, come back again, like mere motion will give me confirmation.

After a few hours, the general manager himself comes in and makes it official. Randy Mueller tells the media relations' staff that they can release the news that the team has signed Darrin Smith, a veteran line-backer formerly of the Seattle Seahawks, and waived Amp Campbell. Mueller then turns over to me and says, "He's one of your guys, right?"

"Yeah," I say. But why, oh why Amp Campbell?

"Amp was a corner in college," says Mueller. "We tried to play him at safety here."

Tried? He played it for one day.

"We knew he was gonna be a little bit of a project to make the switch," Mueller continues. "We just got guys that are ahead of him right now." He says Amp is probably a little too slow to play corner in this league. "Athletically, he's more suited to be a safety."

Mueller claims Amp's medical condition was not a factor. I doubt this, but he seems sincere. One has to wonder, though, if the Saints didn't second-guess their decision to pass him medically when so many teams were too scared of his injury to even give him a look.

I ask Mueller where Amp is now. He says Amp's in the process of getting a physical and signing a release form. The team makes waived players do those things to prevent the player from having any future injury claims against the organization. Mueller tells me that Amp could be gone by now. So I drive down the street to Ellender Dormitory, and, sure enough, Amp is seconds away from leaving.

He is climbing into a gold Ford Explorer, and if I want to talk to him, I will have to follow this hearse to the airport. Amp appears to be very subdued as he nods at the driver and pulls the passenger door shut. His reaction seems too similar to Carlos Posey's — a quiet shock.

Riding along the bayou, passing under the Lafourche Crossing train trestle, I stare at the hearse and get a sick feeling in my stomach. I feel bad that this happened to Amp and really bad that it happened here. This is where I grew up, a place that has given me so many good memories and continues to make life sweet. Unfortunately, Amp's memories of the bayou country won't be so pleasant. Bayou Lafourche is like the Bayou of Bad Tidings to him. It's the site of a hot hellhole that never began to deliver its promise.

There's something else I'm feeling rotten about, but I have to admit it. If they had to cut one of our 10, I wish it'd been Robert Brannon. It's easy for me to think this because I haven't really sat down with Robert yet and gotten to know him. But I do know that he's the one who came into camp overweight and out of shape. He's the one who only started playing football in junior college. The dream can't burn as brightly for him as it does for Amp Campbell. He can't want it as badly. He couldn't even lay off of the French fries.

When the hearse hits Highway 90, its driver punches it, but there are too many lights and cops for him to maintain his speed. A few minutes later on I-310, he floors it again. The hearse whips around a car at 95 miles per hour, and it dawns on me. *He's trying to lose me.* I realize two things at this point. One, it's not exactly great publicity for the Saints for a writer to get comments from a released player. Two, Amp may not want to talk to me. He hardly even knows me. At this point, though, there's no turning back. This is an ugly side of the story that must be told.

So when the hearse stops to drop off Amp, and the mortician tries to dissuade me from going any further by telling me, "His plane leaves in a half an hour, you know," I ignore him and ask Amp what airline he's flying. I then hustle over to the garage, park and huff and puff through the airport toward Amp's gate.

When I catch up with him, he's still subdued. He'd received the news at 8 a.m. when he was walking into the weight room for the morning's lifting session. Some guy he'd never met pulled him off to the side and told him he'd been released. The guy was brief and to the point. Before Amp had a chance to think about it, he was in a whirlwind, turning in his playbook, taking a physical, packing his bags, heading off to catch a noonish flight. He didn't even have a chance to talk to a teammate.

"I was very surprised," he says. "You work so hard, and you go out there, do well, and the media sees it, and you see it. And you just go out there and think you'll be here for awhile, and look, one minute you're here, and the next minute you're gone."

He had no idea he'd be gone this soon, but it was in the "back of his mind" when they moved him to safety. "I at least thought if you give me an opportunity to see what I can do in the scrimmage or see what I can do in the preseason games, and, I mean, that didn't even happen."

Indeed, Mueller will admit to me a few weeks later, "It probably wasn't fair because he never really got a chance to show Amp Campbell."

Amp knows it wasn't fair, but he doesn't want to harp on the negative. "I done been through worse," he says. "Most people don't even get this opportunity. I mean I'm just blessed." Over and over, he says that this recent development is "probably the best thing that ever happened to me."

I sit there, and I silently wish he would get angry at the Saints for jerking him away from his family, building him up, then tearing him down, quickly sending him home a defeated man. I want him to bitch about why the Saints signed him to a free agent contract if they weren't going to give him a chance to go through camp, when at the time he signed it, he had other offers he could've taken, when now, because of his medical condition, no one is likely to give him a chance.

But Amp's not going to show any anger, at least not in front of me. He'll only focus on the future. "I'm not a quitter, you know. I think I'm a survivor. I'll find my place somewhere in this league. If not, I'll just move on and find me a nice job somewhere."

The somewhere Amp is headed now is home to East Lansing. It will all be better when he sees his daughter, when he can read *Goodnight Moon* to her, as he does every night. But for now, he's got to endure a long, lonely plane ride toward a future that, once again, may never include football.

~

The man who gave Amp the bad news has been called several names. He's known as the Turk, as the Grim Reaper, and as Igor the Executioner. His potential targets don't really care that his real name is Rick Thompson or that his official position is Director of College Scouting. It doesn't matter to them that he's got a wife and two kids. It doesn't matter to them that he may be a decent man.

They only know him for what he can tell them. They only think about how his words can end their careers and put their futures in doubt. They only see his strong facial features, his icy eyes, his steely gray hair. They only see Igor the Turk.

Igor has been turking for a long time. Before coming to the Saints this year, he turked in Seattle for 13 years. For all of those years, he and Randy Mueller worked together in the Seahawks' front office. When Mueller hired him in New Orleans and asked him to turk again this year, he agreed. In fact, if he's forced to be the Turk for the rest of his NFL career, he doesn't have a problem with it.

"Certainly, it's a difficult job. Nobody likes to do it," he says. "I don't think anybody in an organization likes to go tell a player that they're no longer sought by the organization. But you know it's a business. The players understand it. The staff people understand, so it's not nearly as traumatic as you think."

Yeah, Turk, not as traumatic as *you* think. He admits, "You become numb to it a little bit." He says there have been times when it was tough for him to bear the message. These are the instances where he'd been around the player for years, like former Seattle quarterback Jim

Zorn. But in most cases, the attachment just isn't there. Most of the time, he can lower the guillotine without emotion.

The protocol for this year's camp will be for him to simply tell the player that Coach Haslett needs to speak to them. Amp's case was unusual because the Turk himself told Amp he was released. This is not supposed to happen again, but the Turk's message will nonetheless be clear. "When they're told to see Coach Haslett by me, I think they all pretty much understand why."

And to know why is to know the rules of this "game before the game."

~

Back at Nicholls State that afternoon, the players don't know why the Turk tagged Amp Campbell. Most of them don't even know that it happened. In fact, some won't even know that he ever came to camp. Looking at campus now, it doesn't seem that anything unusual has taken place. An hour before practice, the place is a flurry of activity. In every direction, four-wheel Kawasaki Mules buzz, and golf carts scoot. They carry Saints executives, coaches, and in some cases, players. The carts are driven by what seems like an army of crew-cut young Saints' staffers and in other cases, by some of the dozens of Nicholls students who have been hired to work the camp. The players themselves aren't allowed to drive them. It's another sign of Coach Haslett's phobia of injuries. "I just don't want somebody to get hurt with the gravel out there, just the conditions," he says.

The conditions for the three o'clock, one-a-day practice are feverish. With the heat index climbing beyond 110, it is decidedly hotter than yesterday's morning session. Despite the intensified swelter, practice hops like grease in a skillet. The scene is organized pandemonium. Just as the players settle into one drill, the air horn blows, and the players hustle toward another drill. They must run between drills, or they will be fined. Practice moves like basketball, soccer, or hockey. It's not methodical football. It's not even no-huddle football. For the rookies, these first few practices can be confusing. "It's like everyone's talking all the time," says D.J. Cooper.

~

One person talking now is defensive coordinator Ron Zook. He yells, "Let's go. Let's go. Come on, let's go to work here."

Zook is always working and always going. He is constantly moving, shifting, maintaining a fast, chest-out strut like a rooster hopping around the barnyard. His mouth flaps constantly. He trash talks the offense and never ceases instructing, praising, or chastising his defense. His tee shirt is always the first to become soaked through with sweat. It doesn't matter. He never seems to tire.

While Zook's stamina is shared by his boss Haslett, the head man is not nearly as frenetic. His demeanor is laid-back yet attentive. His long, loping stride is always hovering near the huddle. He keeps his short, thin, neon-bleach-blonde hair tucked under a baseball cap. His frame is sinewy, taut, and towering, and his shoulders are slightly crouched as if he still wants to get in his old linebacker's stance, the one he used as a former Buffalo Bill back in the late '70s and early '80s. He may be a rookie head coach, but there's no doubting he's the man in charge.

"He has the persona about him, you know, he's a head coach," says Pete Destefano. "People respect him. He's been a player. He's a kind of no-nonsense-type guy. You know what to expect out of him."

The head man's expectations are what Pete is trying to exceed. Now that they're practicing in pads at least once a day, he's jacked up. The contact is what drew him to playing safety. "I like the fact that there are alleys," says Pete. "You can blow people up."

Near the end of practice, a bucking horse of a ballcarrier named Wilmont Perry comes rumbling down an alley, and Pete reacts. He squares and does his best to blow up Perry. The thud is the loudest thus far in camp. It's loud enough to send tremors into the cane field. It's also hard enough to push Pete's face mask against his nose and leave a gash that will require three stitches. Zook sees the hit and slathers. He runs toward Pete and gives him a high five.

Having seen the blow from the media area, Mike Detillier comes up to me and says, "Pete stuffed the run! He stuffed the run, podnah."

~

As big-time a stuff as it was, the Saints' coaches already knew that Pete was a physical player from watching the tape of his thunderous hits at Cal. While they are pleased that he is proving his physicality, their questions are about another part of his game. "The thing that is going to be interesting about Pete," says Rick Venturi, "is how he's going to play in the deep part of the field, which he didn't have to do a lot of in college."

Pete has heard the concern about his coverage skills, and he's anxious to prove his mettle. All he needs is the repetitions, the "reps," to prove himself. At present, Pete is technically running third team, and one of his competitors, Eric Johnson, is running fourth. But practically speaking, Pete must share his reps with Johnson on the third team. To an unproven player, reps are like gold. The more reps he gets, the faster he learns, the more chances he has for a play to come his way. Without enough reps, he finds himself thinking too much out there, not reacting.

"It's kind of scary as a rookie," says Pete. "You don't want to go out there and make mistakes. That's the worst thing you can do is go out there and not know how to line up or not know your assignment. It's hard enough just making plays, but then try to make plays and do something that you don't even know what you're doing, you might as well pack it up and go home."

Unlike Pete, D.J. Cooper is getting plenty of reps. The rash of injuries on the defensive line has forced him into more action. Coop sometimes feels like the extra reps are hurting him. "When you're tired, it's hard to think straight," he says. The heat is making it difficult for him to concentrate. "I ain't never been around no heat like this. And I mean, I'm from Texas. I've practiced on turf, you know. Shuhh, that's hot."

After practice and after supper, Coop walks out of the cafeteria with his slick, bald head pointed downward. He speaks much softer than usual. He's hardly acting like the fun-loving, loose, personable guy that he is. Now, the *joie de vivre* has all but left him. He seems a long way from the man who bulldozed Willie Roaf last night. "I didn't have a good practice today. I got yelled at a little bit. I don't like getting yelled at. I just want to play good. I guess I made too many errors today."

When he's asked who yelled at him, he says, "It was the head. He also gave me a compliment yesterday, and I'm really superstitious about compliments. I get a compliment one day; you know everyone's talking good, this and that. Then the next day, I fuck up all day like today, so that's why I don't like being complimented."

Coop's current mood swing matches the rap on him coming out of the University of Arkansas, where his confidence level bounced up and down. "D. J. Cooper is a guy that doesn't know exactly how good he is," says Mike Detillier. "He never played (at Arkansas) like he was a starter. He always played like he was looking to get rotated. In this league you do that, you gonna get unemployed. But he is, to me, the type of football player that if the light ever comes on, and he realizes just how good he is, he can play in this league."

"D.J. is, hey, he's athletic as hell," says his position coach, Sam Clancy. "He's quick. He's tough. And he don't take no stuff from the veterans. You know, he holds his own, and he backs it up."

Clancy says Coop is making mistakes, but all rookies do. Coop's problem is the mistakes are dominating him right now, cluttering his mind as he walks up the road to the dorm. But he's always had a lot on his mind. He's always had the big ol' globe resting on his shoulders. You can't blame a person for feeling that way when one day, he's 17 years old, and his mother dies, and he's never really known his father, and his stepfather leaves, and he's taking care of his little brother and his little nieces, and the bills are stacking up.

$$\sim$$

By 11 p.m., the players must all be safe and snug in their dorm rooms. As one of the coaches walks down the hall for the bed check, he opens undrafted rookie Terrence Miles' door and shines a flashlight on his bed to make sure Terrence is in it. Terrence is in it, all right. He's too tired to be anywhere else. He's endured a day of weight lifting, meetings, practice, and more meetings. In between are meals, but precious little time to rest. Whether it's the one-a-day practice day or the two-a-day, they're equally exhausting.

Despite his fatigue, Terrence smiles. Ever since he first started playing football in the middle of Lambert Street in North Philly, he dreamed of being exactly where he is now. He was a wide receiver then, not the hawking, darting linebacker that he is today. The Saints signed him out of Pennsylvania's Kutztown University for primarily one reason. "I want guys who can run," says Randy Mueller, "and he can run."

By observing Terrence do anything with his hands, his feline quickness is evident. The first time I met him his hand *snapped* when he casually threw a piece of tape toward the trashcan. It was as if Sugar Ray had just flicked a jab.

Terrence's explosive power makes up for his lack of size. There aren't many linebackers playing at 210 in the pros. He's got a collegiate pedigree, too, even though it may not appear that way. Kutztown is also the alma mater of two former All-Pros and potential Hall of Famers, Denver linebacker John Mobley and Washington wide receiver Andre Reed (who spent his best years with Buffalo). Terrence is proud to follow in their footsteps. He's also proud that he's just a few credits away from obtaining a degree in social work and criminal justice.

For Terrence, tomorrow is almost as special as graduation day. It's his 23rd birthday.

/ FIVE /

THE MONDAY GAME

MONDAY, JULY 17, 2000, 6:30 A.M.

The sound of an air horn blasts through the fourth and fifth floors of Ellender Dormitory. The players shift in their bunks and cover their ears. The agitator is Jay Romig, who is usually the Saints' Manager of Information Systems. But at this camp, he is the dreaded alarm clock.

"They (the players) don't like the person that does it," says Romig. "That's for sure. Usually we have one of the young guys on the staff do it. But Coach Haslett wanted me to do it this year. So I don't mind. I'm up (anyway)."

The problem is Romig really does mind. He's no bigger than a leprechaun and doesn't want to expose himself to these monsters. He remembers a couple of years ago when the Saints were training in LaCrosse, some of the players tied the person in his position to a flagpole and left him there most of the day. While this guy was brash, and Romig is polite, he'd rather not take any chances.

"Every now and then you have somebody look out and give you a dirty stare, or they'll get on the elevator with you and give you a dirty stare, but I'm in and out of there too quick for them to get too mad."

However, on this morning, many of the players are mad, Monday mad. Time is starting to mess with them. It's Monday, but it's not really Monday. It can't be when you traveled Friday and worked nonstop Saturday and Sunday. You know you won't see any freedom until this Saturday afternoon, and you feel like you haven't had any for a week.

It's only the third day, but you're extra sore this morning. You can feel the sun in your skin, even in the air-conditioning. It's only been three days, and you're starting to drag. You know you've got to forget about it and play every snap like you've been fired from a cannon.

~

Terrence Miles has no trouble springing from his bed this morning. It's not every day you turn 23 and take a dream-shot at the same time. Sometime before 8 a.m., he's talking on the phone to his mother, who is wishing him a happy birthday. He hears a knock on the door. He opens it and sees a guy he doesn't know. The guy tells him that Coach Haslett wants to talk to him. Terrence feels his heart drop. He picks up the phone and tells his mother that it isn't turning out to be a very good birthday.

He now has to leave the dorm and walk over to Goaux Hall to Haslett's office. He wants to know why he was cut, but it really doesn't matter at the moment. The point is, he's cut. Haslett tells him that the Saints have signed their top draft pick, Darren Howard, and they needed to cut someone to make room for him. He tells Terrence he made a mistake. Haslett says he should have moved Terrence right away to safety, which is a better position for him in this league, but there's no time to develop him there now.

"He just wasn't big enough in the end to take people on, get off tight end's blocks, that sort of stuff," says Randy Mueller. "What we also told him was to go to Canada, play (in the CFL). We're gonna keep our eye on him."

At present, my eye is focused on the elderly Ellender Dorm house-mother. She's heard about the cut, and it makes her face droop. She checked out Amp Campbell yesterday, and here she goes again. "Aww, *cher*, it breaks my heart," she says in her lilting accent. "It really does."

Terrence comes downstairs, carrying his bags. Like Amp and Posey, he seems subdued, humbled. He's very gracious about doing what will be a quick interview. He looks me right in the eye, telling me, "I really feel like I didn't have a chance to showcase my talent to the coaches and everything because I really wasn't getting too many reps at practice, and that was basically the whole thing, that I wasn't getting too many reps. I was not able to show the coaches exactly what I was able to do. And that's the kind of thing that I'm really upset about."

Terrence says he hasn't had a chance to release any frustration yet, but that might change once he arrives at home in Philadelphia. "I'm just relaxing right now, trying not to let it get me too upset," he says about a minute before the gold hearse drives up, and he climbs inside. It's a shame that he won't, like his fellow rookies, get to take an incredible ride through the preseason, going to New York, Jacksonville, Minnesota, and Indianapolis. He won't get to fly on chartered jets, eat fancy meals, and play against Peyton Manning, Curtis Martin, Tony Boselli, and Randy Moss. Instead, this plane ride will be the last one he takes at the Saints' expense.

Unlike Amp Campbell, Terrence had the chance to speak before leaving to his closest friends on the team, offensive guard Tutan Reyes and fullback Terrelle Smith.

"I was just as shocked as he was," says Reyes. "I woke up, and he usually knocks on my door so we could walk out to practice together. He walked out, and he was like, 'I'll see you later.' I was like, 'What's going on?' And he's like, 'They cut me.' I didn't know what to say. It's hard seeing him go."

Smith was as surprised as Reyes. He tried to cheer up his friend with some encouraging words. He also told him, "I wouldn't be sitting here, waiting. I would either be talking to some coaches trying to get back on, or I'd be on the phone with my agent trying to get with another team."

Smith means well, but it's easy for him to say these things. He's fortunate enough to come into camp as a fourth round pick who's just received a $305,000 signing bonus and who has been given the starting fullback job. His buddy Terrence had to take a much different path, and while Terrence has called his agent, he knows there are few opportunities in the NFL right now.

~

Terrence's fellow undrafted rookie linebacker Jamal Brooks didn't hear the news until practice. "I realized it once he wasn't out there. I can't really worry about that. In the back of my mind, I was like, 'Wohhh!' You know what I'm saying, they starting, but there's nothing I can really do about that."

The cut actually helps Jamal since he and Terrence play the same position, but when Jamal is asked if a part of him is relieved that there's less competition, he says, "Not really. The guys I'm competing with is the starters, with myself first, then the starters."

~

Jamal knows this isn't really true. He knows he's competing with everyone in camp. He knows that while the team must keep a certain number at each position, when it comes down to whether they keep a seventh linebacker or a tenth defensive back, the better player will win.

Two of the more intense position wars taking place are on the offensive and defensive lines. And the war's battle royal is waged every practice in lineman one-on-ones. This morning, the two orchestrators of the drill are getting in their positions, ready to coach their troops.

On the defensive side, there's skyscraper-tall Sam Clancy. Clancy is an ex-college basketball forward from Pitt who was talented enough to play for Bobby Knight on the 1979 U.S. Pan American team. While Clancy didn't make it in the NBA, he did make a career out of playing defensive line in the NFL and USFL, lasting 12 years. Because Clancy didn't play any college football, he understands what it takes to learn the game from ground zero, and he loves teaching every step. As he instructs, his friendly eyes dance, and his arms and shoulders bob and weave, like he's still trying to get to the quarterback.

While Clancy towers over his pupils, the significantly shorter Jack Henry crouches as he teaches his offensive lineman. It's as if he's about to make a block. Henry's eyes show the wear of 14 coaching stops in over 30 years, but his enthusiasm for the game is still apparent. He particularly enjoys the one-on-ones. "I am really, really interested in how they compete," says Henry. "You know if a guy loses, how does he do on the second time around? You know, if a guy's got a guy that he just has a hard time with, how does he deal with that? Because ultimately this comes down to a lot of one-on-ones."

As Henry lowers himself to get a good view of the next round, veteran center Jerry Fontenot prepares to block undrafted rookie nose tackle Desmond (pronounced, "Duh-mond") Gibson.

Clancy hollers, "Make sure you go full speed, Desmond." Clancy is not only instructing his student, but his third cousin. They're both Pittsburgh natives and ex-Pitt Panthers. Despite the relation, they never met until Desmond signed with the Saints.

A coach barks out a snap count, and Desmond fires into Fontenot. Fontenot quickly gets his hands inside of Desmond and holds him at bay. During round two, Fontenot handles him again.

Watching them, Desmond's line-mate, Jared Tomich, says what just happened, a rookie d-lineman being subdued by a veteran o-lineman's snatching hands, is typical. "They get 'em on you so fast. They're really just big hooks, 'cause once they touch you, you're not going anywhere," says Tomich.

Desmond knows that he must learn to immediately knock away his opponent's hands, but he doesn't have much time to study. He's one of three undrafted rookies competing for a spot on the d-line, with the emotional D.J. Cooper and the baby-faced Robert Brannon being the others. "You know you can't keep all three," says Clancy, "but one of those guys has a chance to make the team, and it's whoever wants it most."

During the next round, D.J. Cooper appears to want it too much. Before the ball is snapped, he erupts. Clancy quickly shouts to him, "You jump offsides next time, just back up and someone else is gonna take your place."

While Coop is a little overzealous this morning, some extra zeal would help Robert Brannon. After missing the first day of practice due to the mild concussion, he's already behind the others. He lines up against Tom Schau and waits for the count. What he will do is fairly predictable. He will undoubtedly try to bench press Schau, using his abnormally strong upper body. And sure enough, he thrusts right into Schau and effectively power rushes him. However, on the next round, Schau reads his move and locks him up.

In Clancy's opinion, the battle shows the work-in-progress that is Robert Brannon. "He's really raw," says Clancy. But he adds that Robert may be the most talented of all of his undrafted rookie linemen. "When he do it right, he's a stud."

"He's a little bit top heavy in that he's tremendously powerful in the upper body," says strength coach Rock Gullickson, "and I think he kind of gets his body out in front of him sometimes, and he can't keep his feet underneath him. Once he harnesses all that power and has the agility to move his body around like he needs to, he could be something special."

There are special reasons why Robert hasn't quite figured out how to harness all that power, power that has resulted in his number one rookie bench press of 405 pounds. Up until two years ago, he'd hardly ever been in a weight room. Up until four years ago, he'd never played one down of organized football.

∼

Robert Brannon's hulking frame supports the face of a 15-year-old. His expressions and mannerisms are often childlike. His naiveté is funny, pleasant. "Isn't he great?" says Pete Destefano. He certainly has a great quality, whether it's humility or lack of self-awareness, he comes across as that rare, quiet man-child that has no idea how good he can be. He wouldn't know pretentiousness if he tripped over it and landed in it face first.

Despite his innocent appearance, Robert didn't have the most innocent of beginnings in Carson, California. His father, Berthold Brannon, was in and out of jail throughout his early youth. When Robert was in the fifth grade, his father was stabbed to death while someone was trying to rob him. Sadly, Robert never really got to know him.

Robert says growing up in his inner-city Los Angeles neighborhood was "not too nice." But except for some fighting problems in elementary school, Robert stayed clear of trouble. His mother, Darlene Hampton, who raised Robert and his three siblings as a single parent says Robert was "sheltered." She says he "didn't hang out a lot." His friends were mostly associated with sports.

All through his adolescence, Robert's only real sport was basketball. He starred at forward for Rialto High School and later signed up to play hoops at San Bernardino Valley Community College. "I wasn't thinking about football at first," he says, with a slight lisp. "I was thinking about playing in the NBA. I don't know. Something just turned my head, I guess. I don't know what it was."

Robert had no intention of playing football until one of the San Bernardino football coaches spotted him registering for classes as a freshman. The coach asked him, "Do you play football?"

"No," said Robert, "I play basketball."

"You're big enough to play football. Why don't you try out?"

"I said, 'Sure.' I don't know why I said that. I just did. I went out there. I didn't know nothing about football, nothing about no d-line or anything. I just saw it on TV. I don't know how I came, how I played football. I don't know."

The new sport was initially an adventure for him. "The first time I got into a game was a punt return on special teams. I didn't know what to do. I was just running down the field, not hitting nobody, just running down there like I'm racing somebody. My friend asked me what I was doing out there. I said, 'I don't know.'"

Robert didn't play much his freshman year, but when he returned for his sophomore season, he became a starter. He then decided to play football only. "Why did you give up basketball?" I ask him.

"I don't know." He laughs. "I don't know."

"Did someone say, 'Robert, your future lies in football. You can make a lot of money playing football one day. In basketball, you'll never be a pro.' Did anybody tell you anything like that?"

"No, really, people ask me why don't I play basketball, now."

After an All-Conference season his sophomore year, Robert was nationally recruited. He ended up accepting a scholarship to Iowa State and decided to major in sociology. As a Cyclone, he made steady improvement, and after his senior year, he expected to get drafted. Mike Detillier projected him as a 6th or 7th round pick.

In April, as the draft rolled into the fifth round, teams started to call his agent, hoping they could sign him if he survived all seven rounds without being selected. So many teams called that Robert can't remember them all. "Why," I ask him, "did you pick the Saints over the other teams?"

"'Cause to be honest (in New Orleans) I didn't have to be in no super cold weather." He says the organization and the coaches weren't really a factor. He simply wanted nothing to do with snow and freezing rain.

When Robert is in balmy L.A., his mother says he's a playful person. He likes to hide in the house and scare people who don't realize he's inside. He loves to hum the Star Trek theme until he drives his family crazy.

Not everything in his life, though, is playful right now. His girlfriend Stacy Anderson, who lives in Big Bear, California, is pregnant with his child. The baby is due in about a month. He's pretty nervous about it. He knows everyone would be better off if he made the roster and earned the $193,000 rookie minimum this year or made the practice squad and earned $64,000. It would sure solve a few problems.

Robert says he hasn't thought about the cuts at all. He doesn't even realize at this point that anyone's been released. Maybe, it's better that he stays blissfully ignorant. They say if you dwell on the negative, you'll cut yourself.

~

As Pete Destefano takes the field for the night practice, being cut is the last thing on his mind. "I really think I'm going to make this team," he says. He says this even though two of the coaches yelled at him during the morning session. It happened when he ran toward the line of scrimmage to provide run support, and the ballcarrier slipped in front of him and fell to the ground. Thinking the play was dead, Pete walked away.

Zook charged in his direction, "You gotta tag him! You gotta tag him!"

Venturi was on his heels, yelling, "Where'd you go to college?"

"You're not in college anymore, Pete," hollered Zook.

Under college rules, a ballcarrier who falls to the ground by his own doing is considered down, but in the NFL, the runner must be tagged, or he can get up and continue to run. In this case, Pete didn't tag the ballcarrier because the ballcarrier had slipped out of bounds.

Later, Pete says that Venturi approached him and said, smiling, "Dog, you didn't tag the runner because he was out-of-bounds, huh?"

"Yeah, that's why I didn't tag him," said Pete. "But I didn't want to tell you guys anything. You're not supposed to talk back to the coach."

"Yeah, dog, you were in the right place, and you did the right thing.

That's why you'll probably be here when the season starts."

These words are like tonic to Pete. He knows things could change. He knows Venturi can't make him any guarantees, but at least, someone has confirmed he's doing well. At least, all those nights of coming home after the spring coaching sessions and studying his homemade flash cards are starting to pay off. At least all those days of killing himself in the gym making his triceps bulge count for something. He can play a little more loosely tonight. He can feel a little surer of himself.

He can even start to block out what happened to Amp Campbell, who was his locker mate and fellow defensive back. Before the first night practice in warm-ups, he and Amp took turns helping each other adjust one another's pads. They were joking and laughing, then, bang, the next morning, Amp was gone. "It affects me," says Pete. "I don't know about the rest of the people. It's funny. I think only one other person's even made a comment about it. I still haven't gotten over it yet, really. I know that's one of the first of many people who are going to be cut."

But Venturi's words have helped him not think about the ever-looming cuts. He can practice now, really practice.

During that night's practice session, in an 11-on-11 drill, the ball sails high into the air, heading toward wide receiver L.C. Stevens. Stevens jumps, and as he does so, a defensive back lights into him and knocks him to the ground. He doesn't move at first, then his leg starts flapping like a dying animal's. It is flapping wildly. The trainers run to his aid.

As his leg flaps, as he winces in pain, the drill doesn't skip a beat. There is very little pause. There is no real observation of the fallen. Without much hesitation a coach signals for the entire offense and defense to move further toward the end zone, so they can scrimmage away from the site of the injury. The trainers attending to Stevens look up a few times as if to make sure they're not in the way.

To some observers, this whole scene is kind of shocking. It's not like during a game when an injury brings everything to a halt. Later, they'll find out that Stevens has a fairly minor shoulder injury. But at the moment, no one knows that. All they see is a man with the leg flap of a dying deer. It's as if nothing is too important to stop practice. Nothing is worth missing a single rep. There is too much to do to prepare this team for the season, for that opening game against Detroit. Not one ounce of preparation can be lost. Concern and respect for the injured must not be shown until practice is finished. Like they say over and over and over, this is a business, and the business comes first.

~

When Chase Raynock returns from practice to Ellender Dormitory around 10:00 p.m., he's worn but wired. His legs are Jell-O, but his mind is racing. There's not much for him to do in the hour before curfew, except maybe scarf down a large pizza. He can't afford to leave campus and risk missing bed check. Moreover, he's spent. He would like to just crash, to soak up as much sleep as he can before the 6:30 a.m. horn sounds. He had no problem sleeping the first couple of nights when he was too exhausted to do anything else, but now he's getting used to the schedule.

"Some nights you start thinking about what you did that day in practice, and it starts wearing on you," says Chase. "It makes it hard to go to sleep, you know."

Sleep is made more difficult by the lack of a blanket. A Montana man like Chase is used to one. He needs more than the two little sheets he was issued. He says he'll get one this weekend, but for the time being, books will have to keep him warm. He's a voracious reader, especially of science fiction novels. He's read all of the "Stars Wars" books, and this week is conquering Rick Shelley. He's churning out almost a book a day, using some of his short midday rest time to read. Some nights, as he becomes immersed in an otherworldly adventure, he finds himself saying, "Woah, it's midnight, I better go to sleep." Then the day's performance starts swirling in his head, and sleep becomes only wistful.

While Chase reads to "wind down," some of the other undrafted rookies kick back by playing Ping-Pong in the lobby, playing video games, watching TV, or calling girlfriends, friends, or family. Every night, D.J. Cooper calls home to Fayetteville, Arkansas, to his wife, Stacy, and to his 11-month-old daughter, Dallas. Talking to his wife, however, doesn't relax him. He finds himself rehashing the mistakes that he made that day in practice. When he asks her about her day, it gets worse.

"We're broke right now," says Coop. His wife is looking for work but is discouraged because it's difficult to get a good job when she must tell her prospective employer that if her husband makes the team, she'll be quitting in six weeks. Meanwhile, Coop is waiting for his two weeks in camp to elapse so he can get paid (the gross pay is $700 per week) and send some money home.

Lately, the "furniture people" have been showing up at the Coopers' Fayetteville apartment to reclaim their leased couch and love seat. "They haven't got it (the furniture) yet because we ain't opening the door," says Coop.

The talk gets so depressing that Coop tells his wife, "Put Dallas on the phone." He listens to his daughter goo and gaa and let out a long string of "Da, Da, Da." He laughs, but when he hangs up the phone, he can't seem to turn out the lights. He won't deal with another night of tossing and turning. So he takes one of the sleeping pills that was given to him by a trainer. He hopes the pill will do what nothing else can.

/ SIX /

STARING DOWN THE FRANCHISE

TUESDAY, JULY 18, 2000, 6:30 A.M.

Rubbing their eyes, the players stand in a long line at the Barker Hall locker facility. They are waiting their turn to have a doctor watch them urinate into a cup. With this drug test, no chances will be taken. The team won't allow a player to pee in private and do something to alter his urine sample.

Normally at this hour, the players would be in their bunks listening to the air horn. They could wait 'til as late as a few minutes before 8 a.m. to run over to the cafeteria to check in for the mandatory breakfast. Instead, they've lost those cherished winks. They must now endure a little embarrassment and deal with the fact that this day will be even longer.

When the players finally make it over to the mess hall, they are greeted by an ominous headline in this morning's New Orleans *Times-Picayune*. It reads, "Searing Heat Kills 4 in State." It seems ludicrous. Four people in Louisiana have just died from heat-related causes, and these men are going to put on heavy clothing, go out at the hottest part of the day, and bang against each other for two and a half hours. Of course, the people who died from the heat weren't surrounded by trainers, a sports medicine staff, water boys and readily available Gatorade, bottled water, and intravenous fluids.

"The great thing that Coach Haslett does with the team is he allows them to drink practically at any time during practice," says strength and conditioning coach Rock Gullickson. While he says Haslett doesn't allow any mass water breaks, he adds, "If you're taking three reps, you're probably going to go, one, two, three and then come out right away and get something to drink."

In addition to inundating the players with fluids during practice, the Saints' staff takes other precautions. Gullickson and his assistant, Evan Marcus, maintain a daily log of each player's body weight. The players must weigh-in before and after every practice. If a player loses five pounds after one session and fails to regain it by the start of the next session, he will be held out of that practice. "They might drop six or eight pounds, but most of them will replace that in between practices." He says the "big guys" may "drink a gallon of water per hour (during practice) and still lose 6-8 pounds."

Sometimes, even with all the available fluids, a player doesn't drink enough water, and the result is dehydration. One player who has experienced it is wide receiver Ryan Thelwell. "It's scary," says Thelwell. "You've had cramps in your legs? Just picture it going all the way up to your neck, and your body just tightening up."

"A cramp in your calf can lead to a cramp in your quad to a cramp in your abdomen. It can be like a forest fire almost," says Richie Naquin, a registered nurse who is working the Saints' camp as an IV tech.

"It's kind of like being paralyzed," says Thelwell. "You can't walk. You can't move. You're dizzy. You start sweating. It's an intense pain. You just kind of gotta bite down and just kind of hold it off. They have to carry you into the training room to get IVs."

Once the IV fluids, usually saline solution, travel into your veins, you start to feel gradual relief, but the effects will linger after the cramps have gone away. "After a few hours, your body's going to be sore from all the muscles tightening up," says Thelwell. "It's not a good feeling."

It's a feeling the players hope to avoid at today's practice, which is being held in conditions that are, as always, ripe for dehydration. Near the end of the session, Chase Raynock has consumed enough fluids to fill a bathtub. He's managed to stave off cramping and while he's tired, he's feeling fairly good as he lines up for a final round of one-on-ones against defensive end Darren Howard.

On the first rep, Chase quickly gets his hands inside of Howard and holds him off. On the second, Howard uses a windmill move to blow past him. Just as Howard comes to a stop, the horn sounds, and the lineman thunder off toward another drill. But Chase isn't going anywhere. He's squatting and holding his chest. He looks like he's either mad at himself, or he's in pain.

A few minutes later, practice ends, and Chase sets the record straight. "I got hit in the sternum. My sternum is really sore right now. I'm having trouble breathing here."

Chase's pain appears to be legitimate, but the issue is whether he can legitimately play in this league. Given, he is a Bitterroot Mountain of a man. "He's a big guy obviously," says Randy Mueller. "You can't find tackles like that that don't get drafted."

Despite Chase's size, he seems too nice to play the violent professional game. Granted, there's nothing wrong with being a genteel giant. The world can't have enough nice guys, nor can the league. The NFL is so full of felons that an entire book was written on the subject, *Pros and Cons: The Criminals Who Play in the NFL*, by Benedict and Yeager (Warner Books, 1998). So the more gentle guys in the league, the better. It's not that there aren't nice people playing offensive line and succeeding in the NFL, but when these congenial guys line up, their mean streaks emerge.

Chase doesn't seem to possess the requisite viciousness. "When that ball's snapped, for that four or five seconds, that guy across from you, you hate that guy." That's what he says. But so far, it hasn't come out.

What has been very apparent, on the other hand, is proof that he can pass block. That's what he did most of the time at the pass-happy University of Montana. He didn't, though, do a lot of run blocking, and it's evident. Mike Detillier wrote in his draft report, "Chase is not a real 'root them out' type run blocker and he needs to get a better push up front."

Chase lacks that "push" for good reason. "He is very much behind in his strength level as compared to the rest of the offensive lineman," says Rock Gullickson. In addition to trying to catch up in the weight room, Chase is also learning a new position. For the first time in his life, he is playing guard. Before training camp, he'd been a tight end in high school and primarily a tackle in college.

In addition to changing positions, he's had to adapt to changing geography, from the big sky to the bayou. "I'm used to not seeing a lot of clouds, you know," says Chase. "It's weird over here. The clouds move real fast. They're closer here."

He could have signed with a team much closer to home, like Denver or San Francisco. He says during the seventh round of the draft, "the phone started ringing, just ringing and ringing." In all, 15 teams called him, but most of the team reps doing the calling were lowly scouts. "The reason I chose New Orleans is 'cause Randy Mueller himself called me." He says that otherwise it would have been hard for him to justify signing with the Saints, a team that has three former first round draft choices on its offensive line, which is rated by one preseason publication as the best in the league.

Line coach Jack Henry doesn't see Chase as being advanced enough to make the final roster but thinks he's a candidate for the practice squad. "He's not the most athletic guy in the world," says Henry. "But he's a good worker."

Working on his game here is something that Chase has readily embraced. He realizes his opportunity. He knows that his father, at 42, has worked his whole life and despite having a good job, he will not come close to earning as a truck parts salesman what Chase will earn if he beats the odds and makes the final roster. Chase believes in using your gifts, and the ability to play this sport is a gift he's had since he first suited up for Little Guy football in Billings, Montana.

As the oldest of five brothers, Chase feels a responsibility to set an example for his younger siblings. Of the elder three brothers, Chase is the only one who didn't drop out of high school. He wants to show the older two, who have strayed, and the younger two, who are only 12 and 10, that success is possible with commitment and hard work.

With four days of camp and six practices under his belt, he's ready for Saturday's Black and Gold Scrimmage. He's ready to streamline his roller coaster week into a smooth performance. "I want to be consistent all the way through. I don't want ups or downs. I want to make sure I do every play right, get every assignment right, get my footsteps right. If I get beat sometimes, I'm gonna get beat, but I want to make sure I do everything consistently right."

~

After each blistering practice, the players consistently and universally switch to a much easier pace. They seem to move in slow motion from the dorm to the cafeteria. Some limp. Some gimp. Some walk with an even gait. But none are hustling. Their flip-flops casually slap the pavement. Their music drifts slightly from their headphones.

Some are more interested than others in their culinary destination. They all have to go there for all three meals per day, or they'll get fined. So while all sign up, some will leave without eating anything. Others will grab a sandwich or a turkey burger and take off. Sometimes, it's because they're too hot or too tired to eat. Other times, it's because they're picky, and they just don't want to eat what's being offered. If they don't like the menu that day, there're plenty of snacks back at the dorm, plenty of fruit, Power Bars and cold cuts. There's also a wide selection of supplements, from creatine to basic vitamins. Every night at 9:30 p.m., in addition to all the other snacks being available, stacks of pizzas are delivered to the dorm.

As for the cafeteria training table, it's all about carbing-up. The goal is to starch the players with carbohydrates. So at every meal, there's always pasta, rice, potatoes, and bread. There's also a salad bar, a dessert bar, a selection of meats and seafood. There is nothing unusual about the food, other than perhaps the presence of egg whites at breakfast every morning and the featuring of a few steak and lobster nights. The menu is prepared by the Nicholls catering contractor, who receives input from the Saints' strength coaches and trainers. "It's an ongoing process to get them to understand exactly what it takes to feed a football team," says Gullickson. "They've been really good at following our advice."

Part of that advice is to avert dehydration problems by eliminating caffeine drinks. By the same token, the food, because of the need to make it low in fat, is not likely to be as tasty as your normal local fare here. Consequently, the gumbo doesn't always zing, and the creole doesn't really zap. Nevertheless, from this critic's perspective, the food is good. It's not a cup of bisque from Boudreaux's or a link of boudin from Bourgeois' or an oyster poor boy from Bubba's. It's definitely not Momma's etouffée, or Bébé's gumbo, or the wife's rice and gravy. But it's still good.

Whether the food is good or bad, one might expect these hardworking, oversized men to eat plate after heaping plate. According to the serving staff, that rarely happens. The servers say the Nicholls State players consume much more than the Saints' players. The young Colonels will routinely eat two to three plates of food while few Saints come back for seconds. There are several reasons why the Colonels are hungrier jacks than the Saints. First, many of the Nicholls players are trying to gain weight, while many of the Saints are trying not to gain weight. Second, the young scholar-athletes are still growing boys, while the professionals are men. Third, the Saints have access to all those snacks and supplements. They don't need to load up in the cafeteria.

One person who rarely fills his plate full of vittles is running back Ricky Williams. While Ricky became the Saints' franchise player when last year's coach, Mike Ditka, mortgaged the team's future to draft him, he is far from its franchise eater. On one occasion, he grabbed a tray and scooted past the entire food selection. Then, out of nowhere, he did a complete about face and asked a server, "Can I have a turkey burger?" When the young man started to place the burger on Ricky's plate, Ricky said, "Can I have this one?" and pointed to another slab. Ricky added to his platter only two more items: two pieces of white bread and a peach.

He ate the peach first.

~

Wednesday, July 19, 2000, 8:15 p.m.

Under the lights at Guidry Stadium, it's a peach of a night. Compared to the boiling morning session, the temperature is fairly cool. The atmosphere is charged. Most of the 5,000 Who Dats in attendance are hooting at one corner of the field. They are watching the "Nutcracker" drill, one of the few exercises where the contact is full go. The object of the drill is for the linebacker to run toward the quarterback without getting cracked by a running back. It is similar to the lineman one-on-ones except the linebacker gets a running start.

As Jamal Brooks waits his turn in the linebacker line, he realizes he will soon be taking on The Franchise. He's heard all the stories about Ricky Williams. Jamal watched the former Texas Longhorn on TV in 1998 as he ran over everyone in the Big 12 conference on his way to winning the Heisman Trophy. At the time, Jamal was toiling anonymously at little Hampton, roaming the fields of a I-AA conference called the MEAC. After the season, while Ricky was brooding in New York City after the Colts selected not him but Edgerrin James as the first running back in the 1999 draft, Jamal was watching at a friend's house in Roanoke, Virginia, knowing he probably wouldn't get drafted, but happy that he would graduate in a month with a degree in business management.

A few weeks later, when Jamal heard that Ricky had signed a multimillion dollar contract, which most people considered to be a bad deal for him, Jamal was putting behind the memory that no team had even offered him a free agent contract.

Before the 1999 season, Jamal picked up a copy of an *ESPN The Magazine* with Ricky and Mike Ditka on the cover. Ricky was dressed in a white bridal gown with Ditka posing as the groom. At the time, Jamal had already returned to the Los Angeles area, where he grew up, got a full-time job as a youth counselor and refused to let his football dream die. Every day, he hit the gym at 6 a.m. and attacked the track by 9 a.m. From 1 p.m. to 10 p.m., he worked his paying job, counseling kids with mental handicaps. His only day off was Sunday, and on Sundays he went to church.

As Ricky Williams watched his largesse collect interest, Jamal made about $600 per week.

When the 1999 season got underway, Ricky and Ditka's postmarital bliss ended quickly. Ricky fought injuries all year, making him a nonfactor. After the season, in a *Sports Illustrated* article, Ricky criticized his teammates, Ditka, Jim Haslett, the Saints' organization, and the city of New Orleans. Around this time, Jamal was trying to latch onto any football opportunity he could find. In March 2000, he was invited to participate in the National All-Stars Football Classic, an all-star game in Orlando for post-college players trying to make it in the pros. The game was held at the same time as the Orlando-based NFL Europe tryouts, in which Jamal participated and tested well. Also during this period, he was drafted by the Houston Marshals of the Spring Football League. Not many of his friends had even heard of the SFL, but he went to Houston anyway.

Then, after a practice or two with the Marshals, the Saints and the

NFL came calling. Jamal's contact with New Orleans was John Bunting, the linebacker coach who held the same position last year with the St. Louis Rams, where Bunting first learned of Jamal. At the time, the Rams didn't need a linebacker so they didn't offer Jamal a contract, but Jamal kept Bunting in mind. When Bunting took the job with the Saints, Jamal sent him a tape of the National All-Stars game and a copy of the NFL Europe report. The Saints were interested and flew him in for a workout.

Feeling nervous that day, Jamal didn't perform well in the 40-yard dash and other nonfootball tests. "When we came down to do the drills that show if you can play football, backpedaling, break on the ball, dive after the ball, they said when it came to the football part, it seemed like you wasn't nervous anymore. You wasn't stiff. You wasn't breathing too hard. I was diving after balls. I didn't drop a ball. I caught all the balls. The GM told me we gonna sign you right now."

Jamal's road to the signing was so unusual the GM and the head coach don't even accurately remember how they got him. Randy Mueller recalls him coming from the "All-America Football Camp or something like that over in Texas." Haslett recollects seeing a tape of Jamal from the "Arena League," but "it wasn't even the real Arena League."

"I know what this kid's gone through to get here," says Bunting. "He is not gonna back down."

At the moment, Jamal is ready to show the crowd that he's not gonna back down to The Franchise. He is staring at the visor on Ricky Williams' facemask. He doesn't even notice the dreadlocks coming out of the bottom of Ricky's helmet. He's not thinking about how the kids have almost run him over at times to get Ricky's autograph. He's not hearing the high-pitched "Ricky, Ricky, Ricky" calls that can be heard after every practice. He is, though, thinking about Ricky. He's not focusing on Ricky's ultrashy personality or his quirky ways. He just wants to get past him, avoid a solid nutcrack, and get to the quarterback.

On the other side, it's another opportunity for Ricky Williams to prove himself. He's heard all the talk about how he can't block. He's heard them say his hands are too small to catch. He's not a complete back, they say. All he can do is run, and last year, he didn't even do that

that well. They've called him a flake, an enigma. He knows it's all bullshit, and this is all about throwing it right back at 'em.

The quarterback barks out a count, and Jamal rockets forward. Propelling him is the dream. "It was never a dream just to play it," he says. "It was to be good. I don't think any kid dreams, 'Oh, I just want to be on the team and sit on the bench, you know, and do special teams.' The dream is everybody chanting your name and seeing you score a touchdown in the Super Bowl. That's the actual dream. So it's all in my hands if I can do what I want to do."

Right now, everyone is chanting Ricky's name. The rookie is bolting at him, but no one is cheering for the underdog. Ricky quickly shuffles into position for the block. The ensuing crack rips up the grandstand.

Jamal feels Ricky's hands snatch the numbers on his jersey. Rather than trying to swim him, Jamal tussles with him, treating it too much like a wrestling match. He's trying to pummel him when he should be shucking him. The goal should be the quarterback, not the prima donna. But Jamal continues to press against Ricky, their bodies twisting back, contorting forward. Jamal finally slams Ricky to the ground. It's a definite takedown, but it counts for nothing. The quarterback has had too much time to throw the ball. Ricky wins. The crowd roars.

A few rounds later, Ricky Williams will prove his blocking ability is no fluke when he shuts down Mark Fields, a linebacker fast enough to chase down wide receivers and strong enough to bench press the Superdome. As for Jamal, his second go-round doesn't fare much better. He hustles, but Aaron Craver, a superb blocker, handles him.

When the air horn sounds, Jamal sprints to the next drill. He has already forgotten his performance in the nutcracker. He will only use it as a learning tool, perhaps as motivation. Jamal, though, doesn't need extra motive. He is a 6-1, 230-pound keg of enthusiasm. He gets on a subject, and he can't contain his excitement. He watches Jimi Hendrix on the tube and sees inspiration. He says Hendrix "set himself apart." "I think that's the ultimate professional," he says, "setting yourself apart." Being a pro is not about causing a "ruckus," but it's about being "a professional of professionals."

He moves from professional singers to linebackers. He talks about Jesse Tuggle, the undersized former undrafted rookie that came out of Valdosta State to become the Atlanta Falcons' all-time leading tackler and multiple Pro Bowler. "He decided to be different," Jamal says. He sees himself in Tuggle, darting around instinctively, making play after play. But he doesn't stop at Tuggle. He starts spewing LBs, "Lawrence Taylor—great playmaker. Hollywood Henderson—flair, flair, lot of flair. Dick Butkus—real mean. Ray Nitschke—Jekyll and Hyde." He's just read Nitschke's book, *Mean on Sunday: the Autobiography of Ray Nitschke* (Prairie Oak Press, 1998). He keeps going, "Mike Singletary— I think he was one of the smartest linebackers I knew."

His face reminds you of Singletary. While Jamal's jaw is squarer, and his eyes are narrower, both wear glasses, both move with extreme alertness and energy. "The guy has an unbreakable will," says Bunting.

"His attitude is what you need," says Keith Mitchell, a Saints' starting linebacker who began his pro career in 1997 as an undrafted rookie. "He's really hungry to be there. He's hungry to play. He's excited every day. He comes in and does more than what he's supposed to. He's one of those guys who's a live wire."

Jamal looks at Keith Mitchell and the other older heads and concludes that they are just like him and his friends back home, except they drive nicer cars. "If they're no different than me, physically or mentally, and (if) I'm working harder, then there's really no stopping me."

Jamal can't stop, won't stop. His juice will keep flowing. Flooding over The Franchise, and anyone else who temporarily gets in his way.

~

Thursday, July 20, 2000, 4:00 p.m.

For Bill LaFleur, a big part of the battle is boredom. It doesn't matter that he's laid-back and doesn't let much ruffle the bristles of his crew cut. The fact is he's a punter, and he just doesn't have as much to do as his nonkicking teammates. His performance, though, must actually be sharper. He has fewer opportunities to show what he can do, and when he finally takes the stage, all eyes are on him. "Every practice is like a game," he says. "It's all about your worst punt. What's the difference between your best punt and your worst punt?

"It's special teams because you make special plays out there. There aren't too many guys that can punt a football. There aren't too many guys who can kick a field goal from 50 yards. So you learn how to focus because your practice might only last five seconds. You know if we got out there to practice today and two-punt, I got out there and punted it twice, that's it. I mean, if I punt one good, I had a good practice. If I kick one bad, it was a bad practice."

Bill knows that no matter how well he punts, it's almost a certainty the job will go to veteran punter Toby Gowin. It really doesn't matter that Bill has more leg than Toby and has at times this week, outpunted him. "The reality of the situation is we just gave Toby a great contract," says special teams coach Al Everest. "It's a tough job taking Toby's job here, but who knows what'll happen? You know Toby could get injured. Something could happen."

"My chances are really obsolete, to be honest with you," says Bill. "This camp is serving about three purposes for me. Number one, it's getting me in an NFL camp, which is basically like if we're sitting in this room, and there's one door that goes out of this room, that door right there, and you want to get two rooms away from here, you got to get through that door first, know what I mean? This is that first door for me. I mean, I'm in an NFL camp. I'm part of an exclusive group of NFL punters and kickers that are in an NFL camp this year, that are going to go to training camp, that are gonna play in preseason games."

It has taken Bill a year just to get to training camp. After playing his last season at Nebraska in 1998, Bill wasn't sure about his football future. Punters don't usually get drafted so Bill didn't get an agent for the 1999 draft. Midway through the 1999 season, Bill hooked up with a Chicago agent named Ken Jacobowski. Jacobowski put Bill in touch with Randy Brown, a freelance kicking coach, who lives in New Jersey, in the Philadelphia metropolitan area. Once a month, Bill flew to New Jersey to work with Brown under the agreement that the bulk of Brown's compensation would come after Bill made an NFL roster.

When not working on his punting, Bill was back in Lincoln, Nebraska coadministering a "shooting preserve" with his friend, Brad Wells. At the preserve, Bill guided customers on pheasant and quail hunts and ran a trapshooting range in between hunting seasons. The job gave Bill a schedule flexible enough to continue to pursue his football dream.

While Bill was kicking around the shooting preserve, the 2000 NFL draft rolled around, and by that time, Al Everest had learned about Brown's prodigy. When the Saints' front office couldn't sign two punters they sought as rookie free agents after the 2000 draft, Everest sold them on Bill. "Bill was the fallback guy," says Randy Mueller. "And I don't think there's any question he's been better than anybody we could've gotten from the draft this year. So he's been a great sign."

It's a great chance for Bill, too. He knows that he's not just trying out for the Saints. In the preseason games, even in practices, others will be watching. "There might be a guy that flies in here today from New York, and he's coming to one practice. And he's never seen Bill LaFleur play. If I'm bad today, he walks away and says Bill LaFleur's no good."

Bill has always been good, not just at punting, but at almost anything athletic. He's a scratch golfer, an ace wing shooter, and at Norfolk Catholic High School in northeast Nebraska, he was a punter, kicker, safety, and an All-State quarterback. Bill's athleticism, says Toby Gowin, is evident in his punting. "It's just effortless," says Gowin. "He really strokes the ball. And he really doesn't have to, you know; with me I'm a smaller guy, and I really have to get everything into it to hit 'em well. But with him, it's just effortless."

"There's a lot of times I talk to people," says Bill, "and they say, 'That kicking, does that just come natural?' And I'm like, 'Oh yeah, a little, I mean I could always kick a ball.' And they'd say, 'Yeah, you must just be born with that. I can't kick at all.' And I was like, 'When I was out in the park at 9:30 last Saturday when the sun was going down, I didn't see you working. You know when I was in the (indoor facility) last weekend when it was snowing outside, kicking in the indoor, I didn't see you in there doing it. So don't tell me that it's all natural, you know what I mean, 'cause I worked damn hard to get as good as I am, and if you worked that hard, maybe you can say maybe I'm a natural punter, too. But you don't work that hard.'"

Even with all of Bill's hard work, he must work even harder. "He's got to get his steps down where he consistently strikes the ball and minimizes those real poor punts," says Everest. "You don't last long in this league with two good ones and a real bad one. You're a lot better off with two good ones and an okay one."

Bill doesn't mind working toward perfection. He's craved a chance to play professional sports ever since his dad used to hit him ground balls every night under the streetlights back in Norfolk. They lived on a steep hill, and if Bill failed to scoop up a grounder, he had to run 300 yards down the hill to retrieve the ball.

"There's that point when you're young, you're like, there's no way I can play in the NFL," says Bill. "You don't realize that people in the NFL are just like you. They're that kid playing catch in the street."

Of course, people in the NFL get paid much more than the average kid. "To say that the money isn't a factor, or something like that, it's hard to do when I can make in one year what it took my dad three or four years to make, working really hard at a great job (at the Nebraska Soil Conservation Service)."

But Bill hasn't received that first $12,000-plus game check yet. That's why every punt is potential profit, every step is a future gain or depending on who's watching, an irreconcilable loss.

/ SEVEN /

A DRAG RACE

FRIDAY, JULY 21, 2000, 9:00 A.M.

There were times this week, when you, the player, didn't know what day it was. You'd forgotten about the beginning and couldn't see the end. You were stuck somewhere in a middle with no boundaries. It's not that you can spot the finish line now. It's still too far to see, but at least a break is coming. There will be a little reprieve tomorrow after the scrimmage. It'll be a good 30 hours or so of no football, no heat, no schedule, no bed check, no screaming coaches.

Then there's the bounty of the scrimmage itself. Finally, full contact. Finally, uninhibited war. If you're an older head, it's old news. But if you're a young 'un, especially if you're an undrafted rook, this is your pineapple. It's *carpe diem* 10 times over.

But to get to tomorrow, you have to get through today. Today has just started, and it's already an eternity. The legs aren't what they were a few days ago. You can feel your whole damn skeleton dragging. The air horn is sounding off at faster intervals or maybe it just seems that way. *Drag racing*, that's what's happening. Ten quick plays of 11-on-11 on the big field, then, "Waaaa!" the horn blows, and the whole set moves to the 70-yard field and does the same damn thing. Or did it just seem that way?

The coaches already know it's a drag race, and they turn it up a notch. When in a team drill an offensive lineman seals off linebacker

Phil Ward, Zook goes apeshit. He yells at Ward, "You got to get off that block. Get off the damn block! You didn't even try." Ward walks back to the sideline dejected.

~

It's an emotional game, and on this day, emotions can easily be triggered. Despite these atmospheric conditions, some are unaffected. Some are beyond exhausted, beyond overheated, but they won't show it. Desmond Gibson is one of these people. He lines up in a one-on-one against Robert Hunt, and Hunt gets him once, and he gets Hunt the next time, but on neither occasion does Desmond's expression change. It rarely does and rarely will. He is grateful for this opportunity, thank you, and he's not going to get worked up about anything. One might expect the son of a preacher man and preacher woman to be appreciative, but not poker-faced, not quiet.

The preacher woman is the Evangelist Lynn Dillingham. She travels the eastern seaboard preaching the message of the church of which the preacher man is the leader. He is Bishop James Dillingham of the Ark Ministry, United Holy Church of America, the oldest black Pentecostal church in the country. The Bishop is not Desmond's natural father, but he has been married to the Evangelist ever since Desmond was a little tyke. "I mean that's my dad," says Desmond of the Bishop. "That's the bottom line right there."

When Desmond looks you in the eye with his round pupils and states in his rich baritone, "That's the bottom line," he means it. There doesn't need to be further explanation, and there won't be. Sometimes, he's short because of his modesty. For example, when asked the amount of his signing bonus (rookie free agent bonuses are generally between $0 to $10,000), he says he'd prefer not to disclose it. Other times, he won't elaborate because it isn't your business. For instance, he says that he and the unwed mother of his 17-month-old son, Desmond, Jr., have a "good relationship," but he won't go into any more detail. And when he says his biological father is "not even worth talking about," that's as far as it goes.

Being private and being the son of preachers seems paradoxical. Then again, there are correlations. The cornerstone of any preaching is faith, silent, trusting, blind faith, and Desmond's faith is unflinching. "Nothing happens without God's glory," he says. "That's just how I feel." He doesn't have to explain why this is true to him. It just is.

Another parallel to being the progeny of preachers is his sense of peace, which is a quality his mother says they tried to instill in him. So while he doesn't evangelize, he does peacefully believe. He brought a small Bible with him to training camp. He often recites to himself his favorite passage, Philippians 4:13: "I can do all things through Christ. His strength is me."

Desmond also draws strength from his son. He hates being away from him and calls him every day. "When it's hot out there, and I walk outside at night, and that heat hits, that's the first thing that comes to mind," he says. "I got a little boy at home that needs to eat. He needs clothes and stuff. So I need to do this so I can make his life easier."

But to Desmond, being out here is about more than money. "This is a dream you know, a chance to play in the NFL. So it's really not as tough as you think to get yourself through it because it's something I've always wanted to do."

The game for him started in an area of the Penn Hills suburb of Pittsburgh called "The Lots." There, he played a "free-for-all-type football" with boys who were much older than his six years of age. But he was big and fast for a six-year-old, and he more than held his own. His mother later realized she had to sign him up for organized football when, as a baseball catcher, he started tackling runners at the plate.

Her instincts were correct. Desmond was so dominant as a nose guard in midget ball that his parents decided to take him out of a private Christian school, which he'd attended from kindergarten through seventh grade, but also where there was no football, and enroll him in the public school system. His mother worried a little about taking him out of a sheltered environment and exposing him to the temptations of a bigger, less monitored place. But Desmond made a smooth transition. "Desmond has always been an individual," she says. "He's never given me a day of trouble. I've never had any problems. He's always been a very mature young man."

His maturity was also evident on the field. He went from starring at Penn Hills High to starting as a freshman at Pitt. Despite starting most of his games during his four years as a Panther, he's now at the very bottom of the rung as a Saint. He's competing against two fellow undrafted rookies, Robert Brannon and D.J. Cooper, as well as a host of older heads. Of the rookies, Coach Clancy says, "Desmond's probably the most experienced out of the bunch."

However, Desmond doesn't necessarily feel experienced in these trenches. "It's just so much faster," he says. He says he's trying to develop "NFL habits." He knows he must develop them now because injuries have opened a window. But they aren't season-ending injuries, and soon, the window will slam shut, unless his new NFL habits keep it open.

~

At the tail end of practice, Pete Destefano sees a hole open up, and a mouse zip into it. It's Mighty Mouse, Chad Morton, the skirting, scooting, skedaddling scatback who has thus far slipped away from every big hit that's come his way. His moves have sent the camp crowds into a tizzy. They've watched him disappear into the land of leviathans and pop out with his cape still in one piece, with his ears and whiskers still intact. This time, however, Mighty Mouse is moving toward one intense Italian-American. This lean, mean cat has rung him up before. Back then, the mouse was at USC, and the cat was at Cal.

The ol' cat wonders if the mouse has muscle memory. Pete remembers it all very well. It's funny how life moves. One second, he and the mouse are both in the sun-washed Pac-10, running all over gridirons up and down the Pacific Coast Highway. They're both BMOCs, both All-Conference. But the mouse has got something that he doesn't—speed wheels. Oh, Pete knows he's no poke. He can outrun the guy at the gym who thinks he's got jets. He says he ran a 4.52/40 for the scouts. But this is a whole new level of stopwatch.

Pete knows that in his gut, it's all *caca*. He blew up the mouse in college, and he blew up the other Pac-10 guy, the Saints' rookie fullback, Arizona State's Terrelle Smith. He's not really sure what sets Smith apart. It can't be the guy's black belt in karate. Heck, Smith didn't hardly play at all for three years as a linebacker, then he moves to fullback for one year, and what do you know, he's drafted.

Drafted. Smith in the fourth round, the mouse in the fifth. Pete starts for four years at Cal, and he doesn't even go by the seventh. It's

his 24th birthday, and nobody takes him. Sure, he had free agent contract offers, and sure, he was happy to sign with the Saints. But still,
"All the hard work I put in, all those months I prepared for the timing
day, and I just didn't really, I don't know, I just wasn't rewarded for it," he
says. "It was kind of like starting from ground zero again."

He doesn't understand really why it happened, but there were
rumors. One was that he had A.D.D., Attention Deficit Disorder, and
people were asking him about "his medication." They'd confused
A.D.D. with A.D., Auditory Dyslexia. Pete does have A.D. It's a condition
that makes it difficult for him to understand someone's speech when
too many people are talking at once. If he's too far away from a person,
he might mix up that person's words with someone else's words. But
this is something he'd remedied as early as high school by sitting on
the front row of class.

It's not a problem now, he says. And you listen to him, and you can
tell he's no dummy. You can see his rhetoric degree from Cal-Berkeley
and take a wild guess that a storied, liberal institution like that just didn't
hand it to him.

So the rumors about his condition probably didn't sink him. Not
even a felony shoplifting arrest could stop Florida State's Peter
Warrick from getting picked fourth overall. It all boils down to
another label placed on Pete. His new head coach even says it: "He
doesn't run real well." Pete is tired of hearing this, and he's also tired of
hearing about why people automatically don't think he runs well. He's
not going to speculate, but he's heard it so much, he wonders.

It's because he's white. "You're too white to run fast." "You're too
white to play d-back in this league."

Pete knows this isn't true. He knows you don't have to be black or
incredibly fast to play safety. He'll point you to Tampa Bay's Pro Bowl
safety John Lynch, a white guy who's lead-footed by NFL standards,
but who's also always there breaking up balls and busting skulls. So
don't give him that white man stuff, just put him back there.

And he's back there now, when Mighty Mouse eyes him and starts
to shift. But it's too late. Pete has somehow managed to run to the
mouse and trap him. How does he even get there, if he doesn't run
well? How did he and Jamal Brooks, earlier in practice manage to close
a Cumberland Gap and knock Ricky Williams back so fast he barely

had time to lower his shoulder? How does Pete now manage to trap the uncatchable, if he's got too much lasagna in his legs? This isn't just a cage that's closing in on the mouse. It's an old-fashioned Acme spring-loaded device. When the bar meets the wood, it makes the trap jump. *Whap!*

The newspapers will call it the hit of the day. But you don't need a scribe to tell you about this guy's physicality. It seems so damn deep-rooted. The roots point to the father, Dennis, the son of Pietro, the immigrant from Italy, who landed in Idaho where he worked in the mines and ended up dying young at age 47. While Dennis didn't follow his father into the mines, he did go the hardscrabble route. He graduated from high school at 16 and stepped right into semipro football for the San Jose Apaches, cracking helmets with 30-year-old men. (Incidentally, the rough and tumble Apaches were coached by a northern Californian known for his mastery of finesse football, Bill Walsh.) After Dennis hung up his cleats, he kept walking the hard edge when he chose law enforcement as a career. He's been in it for 30 years and currently works as an investigator for the Santa Clara county district attorney's office.

"Everything that I did with my dad was physical," says Pete. "That's just how I grew up. It was an Italian family, and that was the way it was. It's how my dad grew up. There was no crying and that kind of thing. If you hurt yourself, it was just get up, rub it off, let's go."

The rough stuff for Pete was innocent at first. He played a game as a three- and four-year-old called "belly bumpers." His father would put a pillow on his stomach, and Pete would run all the way from the other side of his room and plow into him. He'd then fall down and start laughing.

As Pete grew older, his aggressiveness wasn't always laughable. Growing up in Morgan Hill, a suburb of San Jose, he got into his share of brawls in elementary school and junior high. While he wasn't one to look for a fight, he certainly didn't run from them. His father remembers, "I can recall teachers telling me, 'you know he can't fight everybody's fight.' Pete was never a bully. Pete was never a guy to go pick on everybody, but he's never been the guy to back down."

Pete also didn't back down from verbal confrontations with his teachers. "I had a real problem with authority," he says.

All these problems resulted in suspensions, and Pete admits, near-expulsions. But the turbulence at school was minor compared to what was going on at home. "The animosity between my mom and my dad. They have a hatred for one another that's second to none," he says. "I come from a real dysfunctional family."

The dysfunction began when Pete and his sister Danielle were small children. Their father Dennis and mother Marie argued frequently, and the fighting led to separations, then reconciliations, a cycle that didn't end until they divorced in 1994.

During this period, Pete spent his freshmen year in high school with an aunt and uncle in Simi Valley in the Los Angeles area. For the first time, he attended a private school, Grace Brethren. "It was really weird for me because I was at really huge schools all my life. (At Grace Brethren) I went to school with a bunch of sheltered children."

The new environment helped him. He stayed out of trouble and made A's and B's. When he returned to northern California a year later, he attended the parochial Archbishop Mitty High School in San Jose. Mitty provided a sound setting, something he wasn't getting at home. "They (his parents) were still going back and forth, and they were together for my freshman and part of my sophomore years and split up my sophomore year. It was a nightmare."

At the epicenter of the nightmare is this: "I've never been that close to my mother." This is, of course, not usually the case. It's almost always the mother who holds the child's heart. It's almost always the mom that the son clings to, no matter how loving the dad. It's the mom that grows the womb and bears the baby. So it must be confusing when your mom stops celebrating Christmas and your birthday, and you're five years old. It must convolute things when your mom's new religion, Jehovah's Witness, discourages her from associating with non-Witnesses and has her live a lifestyle that your father doesn't live, that your friends don't live, that's nothing like the Catholicism to which you were baptized.

Somewhere along the way, you pick your father or maybe it's your father who picks you. And you still see your mom, and her being a stewardess lets you fly all over and see all these foreign, neat places. But you would give up all those experiences if she could just be your mom, and your mom and your dad could just love each other peacefully under one roof like your aunt loves your uncle.

Above it all, though, above all the bickering and the religious zeal, you still love your mother. If you didn't, you wouldn't get in a fight with your stepdad, who has you arrested, and even though it's a bogus charge, and it's thrown out, you're still bitter, but you still love her even though you must say truthfully, "I don't really get along with my mom too much."

It's impossible for anyone to know if the source of Pete's unadulterated aggression is all the instability, the rejection, and the bitterness. But something drove him during his redshirt, scout squad year at Cal to beat the beans out of the starting running backs and wide receivers. One day, he was punishing them so severely that the coach had to throw him out of practice. This would happen again, later, when he was a starter, and he was just playing football, but the coach thought he was killing the receivers so he got kicked out again.

Maybe it is all of the tragedy that makes Pete a fiendish free safety or maybe it's just his ball-or-bust competitiveness.

Whatever the root of it, Pete has always had *it*. That *it* that separates great athletes from good ones. In his first game for the Pop Warner Morgan Hill Raiders, on a gridiron surrounded by fields of strawberries and apricots, little Pete took a handoff and ran 70 yards. While he dropped the ball before getting to the goal line, it was obvious that the "it" was there. It was there in baseball, too.

He would become a good enough catcher to play at Cal his first two years. Although he preferred baseball, "the thinking man's game," he gave up the diamond to focus on his meal ticket, football, and his future meal ticket, academics.

His current ticket, however, is this team and only this team. Having grown up in the wealthy Silicon Valley, he knows what the team can do for him. He didn't grow up with wealth, but he saw it, was immersed in it. Since coming to New Orleans, he's seen the other side, too. Having driven to the Saints' Metairie practice facility, he felt uncomfortable with the blight on Airline Highway. "I was thinking like, God, I'm going to a place where 90% of the people make a million dollars or more. It seems like the average salary is about a million dollars. And (along Airline) you see houses with holes in the roofs, and a bunch of kids with families who should either be in school or at work, but aren't. They're kind of roaming the streets. They don't look sad or depressed, but it's different than what I'm used to, like seeing a *Forrest Gump* movie or something."

Oh, the legend of Forrest Gump. If only Pete had Gump's speed, he could relax a little out here at practice. If only they were yelling, "Run, Pete, Run," he would've been a first round draft choice, like his d-back mate at Cal, Deltha O'Neil, whom the Broncos selected with the 15th pick. But he's not Gump, and he's not O'Neil. He's a young man staring at Goliath, a man who's a little frustrated because he can't really whack people out here, even though he's just whacked the mouse. He knows tomorrow he'll have the chance to whack 'em all. Finally, he'll really do, whether one calls it violence or vindication or victory, what he does best.

~

By 5 p.m. that evening, I'm doing my best to stay awake. I'm walking away from my last interview outside the cafeteria, and I've about had it. My brain is fuzzy and fumbled. It's feeling the effects of soaking in a bubbling crab boil all week. It's also feeling the wear of dealing with the Saints' pesky media police (officially called "media relations"). Granted, the police serve part of their purpose. They diligently transcribe all of Haslett's press conferences, and they prepared a thorough media guide and helped set up some of my initial interviews.

But, sometimes, interacting with the media cops feels like falling into a red ant pile. When you invade an ant's space, they don't welcome you. They bite you as many times as they can and try to shoo you away. Sometimes, it appears the media police are trying to keep me from getting my story instead of helping me get it; biting me instead of giving me a friendly smile in what is otherwise a friendly town. While ants have a reason to bite the person who has destroyed their home, the media police cannot justify biting people who provide free publicity and who have created the need for the very job that they hold.

Their campground rules are obnoxious enough. We're not allowed in the locker rooms or in any part of the dormitory, not even in the lobby, and we can't talk to any Saints player or employee while he's in the dining room. We're only allowed to interview the players coming off the practice field and going into and out of the entrance to the cafeteria. During these periods, the players are tired, on the verge of heatstroke, hungry, or all of the above, and they want to talk to a reporter about as much as they want to practice in fiberglass underwear. While these aren't the best of circumstances, they're workable because of the players' cooperation.

But then as the week goes on, the media police or their suspicious superiors start to change the rules. At first, you're allowed to stop a player coming off the field. Then, the media cops tell you that you can't do this. Instead, you must request a player through a policeman, but quite often you make the request, and the player is not produced.

At practice, the media cops don't just observe. They prowl. Several times, I've stood behind the restricted line peacefully enjoying a drill. The next thing I know, I hear the static of a walkie-talkie and see a media cop walking a great distance in my direction, not stopping until he's inches from me. When I move to the next drill, he follows me. Maybe, he's worried that I'll charge onto the field and chop a lineman at his knees, or perhaps, I might run into the huddle and start singing the national anthem. What he really fears is that I'll close-line Ricky Williams, jump on him and pin him down long enough to cut one of his dreadlocks to put in my scrapbook.

Once at practice, I decided to sit down. A media cop told me to stand up. I thought he was joking. He assured me he wasn't. He said Haslett doesn't allow the media to sit on the ground because it doesn't look professional. I asked him if I had to put my helmet back on. He gave me a funny look. "What helmet?" he asked.

This week, my media cohorts and I have often said we feel like we're facing issues of national security. The media police and their fearful bosses treat this as if it isn't a game, but a guerilla war. It's not training camp. It's the Manhattan Project. It's not entertainment. It's espionage. I could rant about how the Saints need the media, but they do it for me in their *New Orleans Saints, 2000 Media Information Guide*, which is for "Players, Coaches and Staff." On its cover page, they call the media, "a necessity." They acknowledge that without the media-generated fan interest in pro football, an NFL career "would not be the well-paying career that it is." They admit that they must assist the media "in order to preserve the industry from which we all derive our livelihoods."

To preserve any livelihood that I'm going to derive from this project, I have to deal with the media policemen and their hypocritical oath. I'm sure I haven't seen the worst of it, but I've vowed that I won't let media police brutality get in the way of the plight of our eight heroes.

~

While the media and the players painstakingly labor through training camp, one person here is drifting in ecstasy. He's floating in this Crock-Pot, drinking up every drill no matter how dull the taste. There is nothing monotonous about even padless practices to James Smith. He wouldn't miss a single rep. In fact, he hasn't missed an opening week of Saints' training camp in 12 years. If possible, the superfan wouldn't just attend the first week; he'd be here all four and a half weeks.

His fanaticism defies logic. Just listen to him. His accent is not the Brooklynese New Orleans' Yat, the flat, singsong Cajun or the Mississippi melted butter. It's a drawl with touches of gravel and whine that comes from deep in the heart of another state. James Smith has lived his entire 41-year-old life in central Texas, in the middle of Cowboy and Oiler country. His worship of the Saints began in their inaugural 1967 season. "I guess as a kid I was just fascinated with them," he says. "They were the new team."

Growing up on a ranch in Florence, Texas, James begged his parents to take him to a Saints game, and they finally relented in 1974 when he was in high school. The trip came with a price. "I did a lot of work for 'em, a lot of extra work, lotta chores, everything, especially being raised on a ranch. Oh, I paid dearly to go to that game. I paid dearly."

He has also paid dearly for picking the Saints as his obsessive passion. He has decided to stick with a team that has hired two Super Bowl champion head coaches in Hank Stram and Mike Ditka only to see them fail to produce a winning season in New Orleans. It seems like somewhere along the way James would've shifted. He would've bought a Tom Landry fedora or a Bum Phillips cowboy hat and latched onto the Super Bowl champion to the north or to the Luv Ya Blue AFC power to the south. Instead, he did up his house (now his rental property) in black and gold and speckled it with *fleurs-de-lis*. And he filled his closet full of Saints-styled golf shirts. "I buy every one I see," he says. His latest vehicle is a black and gold Ford Lariat truck, outfitted with Who Dat trinkets.

In 1985, during the start of the Saints' 19th straight losing season, James purchased his first set of season tickets. The trucking company owner hasn't missed a home game since 1989, even though to get there he must drive 100 miles per hour to make it from his home in Round Rock, which is near Austin, to the Superdome in 8.5 hours. After a game, when he leaves the Dome and aims his Lariat west toward the Sabine River, he has a hard time forgetting the scoreboard.

"It's frustrating," he says. "I monitor the Internet daily, and I talk to a lot of people. It's just difficult for me not to say anything because, believe me, when you're on the road all those hours, you have time to go over everything in your mind over and over and over. It's really frustrating to me because I see things so clearly, and I get the feeling other people don't."

The Saints' organization has clearly seen his commitment and rewarded it by issuing him a media credential for training camp the last few years, even though he's not a reporter. With the credential around his neck, James can get as close a view of the action as the media police will allow.

So he analyzes by day, and by night, he sips suds with his podnah, Rodney Henry, team owner Tom Benson's bodyguard. To many, it may seem like a mundane vacation, but to James, it's better than Club Med.

It's one his new bride Dee, who doesn't attend camp, understands. "She realizes my passion for the game, and she's completely understanding, or I never would have married her." He winks and chuckles. "Obviously, she's a great lady."

Lady Dee can only shrug her shoulders. "It's a big part of him," she says. "I realized that when I married him."

Dee doesn't mind having their vacations revolve around Saints' away games. She says she'll be happy to spend their first anniversary in San Francisco in conjunction with the 49ers game, even though the Bay Area will probably be a little cold and damp in December.

But a December day in Frisco is a long ways away from this sultry night in Thibodaux and the smoky Red Goose Saloon, one of many bars clustered among the downtown's creole architecture. The Goose is the site of the town's old post office, which in 1896 became the first one in the country to have free rural delivery.

Saddled up at the historic bar, James smokes a fat stoag and tips a frosty long neck. He's talking up tomorrow's scrimmage. He's bought $10 tickets for as many Thibodaux Holiday Inn employees as would take them. In a second, he's going to walk across the street to Rox's and its Saintsations party. But he'll call it a night soon, being not so much interested in cheerleaders as he is in getting enough sleep to be fresh for the gladiators.

Ahhh, the battle. He would give anything to be on that field tomorrow. It's a dream he had up until he hurt his back while playing defensive back at Texas A&I as a freshman. "Of course, when you see these really professional athletes," he says, "you know that they're one in a million, the ones that actually play the game in the NFL and last any time at all."

Tomorrow, several young men will play the NFL game for the first time. To last any time at all as a Saint, they must make a long, long, lasting impression.

/ EIGHT /

SEMPER FI

SATURDAY, JULY 22, 2000, 10:40 A.M.

This isn't a scrimmage. It's martial law. The men in uniform have set up camp all around Guidry Stadium and have seized control of it from the Who Dats. As the fans in black and gold emerge from their cars, they're greeted by men in combat gear showing off their machine guns and bazookas. The fans soon find themselves eye-to-barrel with a TOW missile system mounted to one of several HUM-Vs fronting the fence. In their periphery, they see tanks and jeeps. And standing at attention is a convoy of helicopters, one from each service branch. There's also a Coast Guard boat resting on a trailer.

The Who Dats move toward the entrance and put a little jig in their step as they hear a familiar tune. A Marine Corps brass band is trumpeting, "When the Saints Go Marching In." As all 10,580 fans march through the turnstiles into the sold-out stadium, they realize that there will never be as much firepower inside as there is outside. Moreover, inside, the troops will be subject to the big wet sun, which is threatening to melt everyone affiliated with the Black and Gold Scrimmage.

In the media police room, there are a few dozen men wearing dress blues and dress greens, posing for pictures with Saints' officials to celebrate some kind of Saints-Armed Forces partnership. Out on the field, the action is about to turn military. For the first time all camp, they're doing form-tackling drills in a sport known as tackle football.

it's narrowing. He says neither he nor Johnson gets the proper amount of reps.

"They should either cut him or cut me," he says in frustration.

Now, Pete has his rep. It's 9-on-7, and that usually means an alley, and an alley means someone to blow up. So when the line blocks down and quarterback Jeff Blake pivots to make a handoff, Pete goes flying down the alley. Blake sticks his hand in the tailback's gut and pulls it out. Oh shit, Pete thinks. *Play-action*. It's 9-on-7, and it's play-action. He looks to his left, and he sees Willie Jackson streaking on a post pattern. The cornerback is tailing him, but he's not close. Pete 'bout faces and boogies. His face is straining, and his hands are pumping, but he'll never catch him. Blake's deep ball is trademark perfect. Jackson's hands are trademark sure.

Jackson crosses the goal line, and the crowd lets out the biggest roar of the night. If the Who Dats didn't hurt Pete's ears enough, here comes Venturi. He's a short, stocky, mustachioed guy, who looks kinda like a walrus. Venturi is charging at him, his jaws are working so fast his head is about to bob off. Venturi fills up Pete's eustachian tubes, damn near makes them explode.

Damn, Pete thinks, can't he see it was 9-on-7, and 9-on-7 is almost always run. I didn't think they would pass at all. But Pete knows he should've been careful. He knows he can't fly down the alley just because the run signs are there. He is deep middle, and just now, he wasn't deep middle. The joy of Monday night's interception is gone. The image of it has faded. Just like that, it's vanished.

~

Thursday, July 27, 2000, 3:30 p.m.

The media cop is calling my name. He's seeking me out. I've just checked into practice, and he wants to talk. Surely, he'll give me an answer about my credential request for Saturday night's Jets game. I made this request at the same time the other reporters made their requests. But the rest of the journalists have confirmed credentials. When I've asked the cop about my credential, he says he has to take it up with the media police chief, who's already in New York.

He tells me now that he's talked to the chief, and the chief has told

"Good hit! Good pop!" barks Rick Venturi. "Have yourself contact ready!"

They'll have to wait for the contact. First, there's a national anthem and a riveting F-16 flyby that shakes the crowd, but fails to cool them. The Who Dats are waving their complimentary gold fans as fast as they can, but out here, they're wax, and wax melts. As the groundlings drip and congeal, the "action" crawls through seven-on-seven and punt drills. Finally, 45 minutes after the "scrimmage" starts, the tackle football scrimmage begins.

Unfortunately, for those trying to make the team, the tackling lasts only for 45 minutes. For the third teamers, the reps are especially scarce.

The undrafted rookies are surprised by the event's brevity. They don't feel like they've had a chance to get into a groove. The highlights include Robert Brannon making a tackle for a loss, Jamal Brooks making a nice open field stop on a screen, and Pete Destefano notching two tackles, including one that took everything he could muster to bring down the buffalo that is Wilmont Perry. Pete's hit on Perry reopened the wound on his nose and required five stitches. He's played football his entire life and has never had that injury, and now he's had it twice in one week.

With the limited reps, some were conservative in the hopes of playing technically correct. "I really wasn't trying to make no big plays or anything," says D.J. Cooper. "I was trying to work on my technique. That come before anything because I can make big plays and still get yelled at."

Chase Raynock found out that despite all the work he put in this week, he wasn't in game shape. "By the fourth or fifth play in a row, I started breathing a little hard," he says.

∼

While it was hardly a real scrimmage, one undrafted rookie, kicker Shayne Graham, was satisfied. He didn't expect any more field goal attempts than he would get in a game, and he delivered on all of them. He found the overflow crowd to be, of all things, relaxing. "Honestly, I'm more nervous when I'm just kicking and there's nobody there," he says.

Shayne prefers there be as many somebodies watching him as possible. This week, veteran kicker Doug Brien kicked in the sparsely populated morning sessions, and Shayne went to work in the heavily attended night practices. "That's what makes it fun, when you know that people are gonna see it. And they're gonna have impressions of you. The coaches are watching, your peers, the players are watching. They've never seen you kick before. They see this little redheaded kid in the locker room. And they're like, 'Is he a kicker?' They don't know anything about me, really. That's just the fun of why I enjoy doing it. If you don't enjoy those types of situations, you shouldn't be in the sport."

The sport began for Shayne as a fifth-grader during one evening in his native Dublin, Virginia. After soccer practice, his father Tom took him out to the baseball field at Riverlawn Elementary, just to see if his son could kick. With the Blue Ridge Mountains looming in the background, Shayne eyed the pigskin in his dad's hold, took a few steps and booted it. The ball sailed toward the top of the backstop, hit the tips of the chain-link, stuck to them, and started hissing.

The deflated ball may have looked like a mangled star sitting atop a Christmas tree, but at the time, Shayne had no idea it was a sign of things to come. He didn't know then that he would try out for the Pulaski County High football team as a freshman, beat out the senior, and that very season hit a game winner in the state semifinals. After that big boot, Shayne never again wore a soccer jersey.

Four years later, Shayne was wearing the maroon and orange of Virginia Tech, where he was a four-time All-Big East selection. His senior year, he helped kick the Hokies to an 11-0 regular season and a berth in the Sugar Bowl/NCAA Championship Final. During that game, Shayne kicked against Florida State's Sebastian Janikowski, who would become the first kicker to be drafted in the first round since 1979.

For Shayne, the draft would be a lot more dramatic than it was for Janikowski. He knew going into it that kickers don't often get drafted. He knew that the NFL was dominated by starting kickers and punters who began their careers as undrafted rookies. He also knew his chances of getting selected would be hurt by the fact that he didn't regularly kickoff in college, and that most NFL teams expect their placekicker to kickoff as well as kick field goals and extra points. Still, because Shayne was projected by Mike Detillier and other analysts as a late round pick, he harbored high hopes.

On both draft days, Shayne decided to play golf with his roommates. He didn't want to put up with the agony of watching the names roll across the television screen, wondering when and if his name would appear. On the second day, Shayne's cell phone rang on the first tee box. It was an NFL assistant coach, but he'd gotten Shayne's phone number mixed up with the number of the player he was really trying to call. "My golf game was shot for the rest of the day after that," says Shayne. "You know, I went the rest of the day waiting for the phone to ring, and it would be my dad saying, 'Seventh round, they haven't called yet.' 'Thanks for telling me, Dad. I didn't need to know that.'

"When I figured out it wasn't going to happen, basically I was just quiet, tried to keep upbeat. I called my agent as soon as the draft was over, or he called me as soon as it was over, and told me he had a couple of people he was talking to, trying to get me signed right after the draft. He's like, you know, I don't think anything's going to happen today, but wait until tomorrow. And then everybody kept giving me the runaround, you know. 'We'll think about it. We'll think about it.' Then it was, 'By middle of next week, we'll have something for you.'"

It took a few weeks before Shayne finally got an offer from the Cleveland Browns to attend minicamp, but not with a contract. By that point, the wait had weighed on him. Almost all of the other rookies knew within a few hours of the draft if they'd be in a training camp somewhere. Shayne had just endured too many days of doubt. "I think my confidence was just down. My head was just not where it needed to be. And I went in there, and I just did not perform."

Shayne left Cleveland and went home to the New River Valley to renew himself. He refined his technique and revived his spirits. His next offer came from the Tennessee Titans, who brought him in for a private workout. There, it seemed like he couldn't miss, but the Titans decided not to sign him.

The Saints were next to call, and something felt right about them from the beginning. He was impressed by how quickly they went through the logistics of scheduling of his workout. "There was no runaround. Everything was professional," he says.

Shayne responded by kicking professionally. "They brought me up to the office as soon as I got out of the shower and told me they wanted to sign me." They didn't offer him a bonus, but he didn't care. Things were finally coming together.

About this time, Shayne's spiritual life was also starting to come together. A few days before he signed with the Saints, he was baptized at the Max Creek Baptist Church near his home in Pulaski County. Shayne's religious awakening had occurred a few months earlier during a conversation with an older friend who was also a member of the church. "He just asked me a question one day about where I was spiritually, and if I died if I knew I was going to heaven or hell. And I didn't know the answer."

Shayne sought the answers by reading the Bible and asking lots of questions. "I got hungry for it," he says.

His continuing spiritual hunger has sustained him during this monotonous first week of training camp. While relaxing in his dorm room, he's read about 1,500 pages of a series of religious books called, *Left Behind* by Jerry B. Jenkins and Tim F. LaHaye (Tyndale House Publications). He's currently learning about Revelation and the end of time.

Shayne knows that his time will end soon with the Saints if he isn't drastically better than the proven veteran Brien. "I wouldn't expect to go into any camp where the kicker, who was there, wasn't good," he says. "My job is not to worry what he does. He can make all his kicks—I don't care. I hope he does. But my job is to prove myself because when I'm out there kicking for preseason games or whatever, there's 30 other teams that are going to be seeing what I'm doing."

~

At the moment, however, the eyes of the NFL aren't on Shayne Graham or his fellow undrafted rookies. The preseason games may be lurking on a not-so-distant horizon, but what's right in front of everyone is a little liberty. Having just endured a week that Jamal Brooks says, "felt like a month," they actually have a short stretch of freedom. They're not due back till a meeting tomorrow at 7 p.m. In the meantime, they're going to close their playbooks and spread their wings. They'll fly somewhere other than the dream fields tonight, even if it's only in their minds.

~

That night, when I walk under the sign at Rox's Bar that says, "*Entrez, Mes Amis,*" the first thing I see is the back of a familiar head. His exposed ears and red crew cut are leaning in toward the bar. He is reaching for something. This is the same unassuming freckled kid that told me after the scrimmage he planned to call his family, read some more of his religious books and sharpen his Ping-Pong skills. He said he wouldn't be hitting the town tonight. There would be no downtown Thibodaux for him.

The freshly baptized Shayne Graham turns around with a few shot glasses in each hand. He notices me and hands me one. A local named Slat grabs another. It's good to see that Shayne has gotten away from his stifling dorm room and his books for one night. He's made fast friends, and he's on his way to feeling the effects of Rox's "Facowee Room." We goose down our shots of the red stuff, and I take a gander around the bar.

A few more of the Saints are here. Chase Raynock is lumbering over to where backup quarterbacks Billy Joe Tolliver and Pat Barnes are sitting. Soon, D.J. Cooper and Robert Brannon will join in the free-beer-for-Saintsfest. They're some of the few Saints that have actually stayed in Thibodaux tonight.

Later on, Barnes and Tolliver hit the bandstand and sing along. They may be battling fiercely for the backup quarterback job, but they're amicably sharing the stage. Chase tries a few times unsuccessfully to grab the microphone from Tolliver. But Billy Joe won't let the rookie have it. Chase ends up hitting the dance floor permanently, and as he bobs and weaves, his shoulders rise above all the locals' heads. A few people ask, "Who is that big dude?"

Shayne's out there duding it up, too. But the bar's owner has got his back. Glenn "Rocko" Caillouet (Mayor Caillouet's cousin) says he's protecting the kicker's golden toe. Rocko tells the patrons repeatedly, "Don't step on his foot."

~

On Sunday, it rains, and the skies stay gray all day. It's so cool it's almost sickening. The players would love for this weather to last until tomorrow, but they just know that it won't. Today, Jamal Brooks isn't paying much attention to the weather. He's doing what he always tries to do on Sunday. "I gotta get that energy for this next week," he says. So he drives an hour and fifteen minutes to New Orleans East to a church that he started attending during the spring practices. He doesn't know its denomination because he's nondenominational. He just likes the church.

Jamal says his goal for the coming week is "to slow the game down more and more." Pete Destefano and Robert Brannon's goal for the afternoon is to take in a movie. I give them a ride to a theater in Houma. As we drive into the parking lot, Pete talks about not wanting to miss the previews, how that's the best part. They've got visions of popcorn and Jujubes in their heads. They get out of the car and walk toward the box office. They look more like kids than they do like pro football players. It's kinda sad that one or both probably won't be around six weeks from now, when the Saints take the field for their version of the big screen.

/ NINE /

THEIR APPLE IS BIG

MONDAY, JULY 24, 2000, 8:30 P.M.

The Guidry Stadium lights are spotlighting a barbaric conflict. It's a struggle for supremacy on the defensive line among undrafted rookies Robert Brannon, Desmond Gibson, and D.J. Cooper. They don't necessarily see it as a battle among themselves. They're just battling, period. But the simple fact is only one, if any, will make this team.

If the deciding factor was sheer upper body strength, the winner would have to be Robert Brannon, the bull with the face of a calf. In lineman one-on-ones, Brannon lines up against Jason McEndoo and jacks McEndoo's chest so hard and so fast that McEndoo *hops* back. From the second Brannon presses him, McEndoo seems to have no control over his movements. His backpedaling is more like an awkward skipping in reverse.

Despite Brannon's brute brawn, he needs to improve his technique and add more moves to his repertoire just as a baseball pitcher must be able to throw multiple pitches. At present, Brannon's only pitch is a hard fastball.

As for Desmond Gibson, the preachers' son has a nice array of moves, but he can't seem to employ them. In tonight's one-on-ones, he's getting repeatedly tangled with the offensive linemen that he's facing. He must shed them faster to be effective. He has been fortunate to run a lot of second team due to an injury to backup nose tackle Robert Newkirk. But at present, he just can't seem to make a breakthrough.

Some days, D.J. Cooper makes real breakthroughs. Others, he regresses. Tonight, he easily swims Robert Hunt, but seems to get lost in his footwork against Jay Hagood. Despite his inconsistency, Coop's talent is apparent. "Cooper's still looking the best," says Coach Sam Clancy. "He's as quick as I don't know what. Once he learns how to play this game, I think he can help us somewhere down the road."

~

The road to an NFL training camp has been a rough, rocky one for Deon Jerome Cooper. Growing up in South Dallas, he says he was a "bad kid" who wanted to fight all the time. If he wasn't fighting, he was trying to do something mischievous, anything for a rise and a laugh. In junior high, he started spending a lot of time in the principal's office, and his mother Evelyn grew tired of it. She told him to take his aggression and his devilish pranks to the football field.

"You see, everybody approach football a different way from me," says Coop. "I think I'm different. I started playing football because my mom wanted me out of trouble. I just did it for her. I didn't think I was gonna get a scholarship or nothing like that. I was just doing it to be out of trouble."

It wasn't that Coop didn't already like football. He'd always wanted to be Walter Payton. But a growth spurt between his eighth- and ninth-grade years made it unlikely that he'd ever become a running back. By this time, the family had moved to suburban Mesquite, and at Mesquite High, Coop found his niche. However, just as his football career took off, the worst tragedy imaginable struck when his mother passed away during his junior year.

Her death was hard on him. "She was my heart," he says. As if her death wasn't difficult enough to deal with, he soon found himself running a household at age 17. "I had my stepfather there, but you know we got into it." They got into it because his stepfather Henry Flowers started seeing another woman less than two months after his mother passed away. He and Coop began to argue frequently. It got to the point where Flowers and his burgeoning drug habit moved out of the house, effectively leaving his teenaged stepson in charge of his natural son, Coop's half-brother, Henry, Jr. and three of Coop's nieces.

Coop had to cook for them, make sure the house was clean, make sure they got on the school bus in the morning. He had to pay the bills, pouring his part-time paycheck from Athlete's Foot and any money he received from friends and family into their care. Eventually, Coop's older sister's mother-in-law assumed care of his nieces, but Coop took care of his little brother until he left for college a year and a half later. At that point, young Henry began to live with his aunt.

Through all of it, the memory of his mother kept him going. "Everything I do is for my mom," he says.

During Coop's senior year of high school, he had a breakout season and was named the National Defensive Lineman of the Year by the *Dallas Morning News*. After high school, at the University of Arkansas, his number one goal was fulfilling his mother's wishes. "My main focus in college was getting my degree," he says. In addition to being just six hours away from earning his bachelor's in criminal justice and sociology, Coop earned the respect of his Southeastern Conferences foes.

But Coop says the SEC doesn't quite compare to the NFL. What's making the NFL more difficult at the moment is a nagging left ankle sprain. He hasn't brought this injury to the trainers' attention. "I ain't never been one for treatment, especially around here. I've learned that if you go in there just to get a little heat on your arm, you know, you might not even be hurting that much, you get a little heat on your arm, and they want you to come at 6:30 (a.m.) the next day. 'All right, be here at 6:30 tomorrow.' Forget that." He laughs. "So I'll just go in there and try to get heat without them seeing or something and just take it over to the defensive line room or something. But if they see you, and you're sitting round in there (the trainers' room), they want you to be there, they want you to be there early the next day and get three times a day and all that. It's (camp's) already time-consuming. I don't want to spend no more time over there than I have to."

Coop says he'll deal with the pain. He'll deal with all the hardships of being undrafted. It's not just because he's had to contend with much worse in his life. It's because he simply wants to be in the NFL. "I want it deeply for myself, badly for my family. It's going to give me the stability that I need for the rest of my life if I do it right, plus, you know, I want to be one of those Pro Bowl dudes, you know, get up in the Hall of Fame, represent my school and everybody that knew me."

~

The Pro Bowl is along ways away from the soft grass of Guidry Stadium, and the Hall of Fame is an almost unattainable destination. For a free safety like Pete Destefano, the action sometimes seems far away from him. On this night, he's out in the deep middle, protecting against the long ball. With the responsibility of being the final safety catch, he can't seem to get into the thick of things as often as he'd like.

Starting strong safety Sammy Knight watches from the sideline and understands what Pete's going through. Along with a few other veterans on the Saints' team, Knight is a model for the undrafted rookies. In fact, he's the paragon. In 1997, he came into Mike Ditka's camp as a rookie free agent, not having the advantage of his drafted fellow rookies, including the second round pick that year, safety Rob Kelly.

Like Pete, Knight is a California native who came out of the Pac-10 as a physical defender who was labeled as being too slow to play defensive back in the NFL. But when the former USC Trojan hit Saints' camp, he benefited from his own surprising performance, and from poor showings by Kelly and some of the veteran safeties. He made the roster, started the fifth game of his rookie year and has been a force ever since.

Knight sees some of himself in Pete. "I think that he's definitely a physical player," he says. "I think that sometimes he gets a little over-aggressive, and he'll have to learn that. That's what all safeties go through. Every safety's been through it, being too aggressive, you know what I mean? But I'd rather have you too aggressive than not aggressive enough. You know, he's gonna be a very good player, and I think that with time, he's gonna develop into a great safety."

It's difficult, Knight says, for a safety to know when he can "steal something" or "go get something" and when he can't. "Sometimes, your competitive juices get flowing, and you want to see that ball, and you want to go after it, but you don't want to hurt your team. Nine times out of ten you'll make that play. But that one time (you don't), it'll go for six."

Knight's lack of great speed doesn't hamper his effectiveness for one reason. He is smart enough to read the quarterback to know exactly where to position himself, to know exactly when to fly toward the line of scrimmage and when to lay back. The sage-over-speed principle becomes more apparent when one studies the position that is "safety of the offense," the quarterback.

The two best quarterbacks in the NFL last year, the Rams' Kurt Warner and the Colts' Peyton Manning, are two of the slowest, most immobile signal callers in the league. However, the mind moves much faster than the feet. And Manning and Warner can think much more rapidly than the most athletic quarterback can run. They can make the initial read at the line of scrimmage, then, once the ball is snapped, go through all of their receiver options much quicker than even the speediest quarterback can scramble and buy extra time. As long as a quarterback's arm is just strong enough, like Joe Montana's, his brain will do the rest.

Consequently, while athleticism is always a huge plus, and a threshold amount of it is an absolute necessity, it's not as important as is a quick mind at a thinking man's position like quarterback or safety.

So at practice tonight, as quarterback Jake Delhomme rolls to his right, Pete Destefano's mind makes a read a million times faster than the world's fastest 40 time. He knows that he's outfoxed Delhomme. He leaves his deep middle and charges for the sideline because that's exactly where Delhomme will throw the ball. Pete's athleticism does the rest. He leaps, extends his arms and snatches the ball out of the air. It is a picture-perfect pick.

He couldn't have chosen a better image to inscribe on the coaches' minds as they walk away from practice. The mental imprint must be as permanent as possible, because in the days ahead, anything can happen.

∼

Tuesday, July 25, 2000, 8:30 a.m.

Today is the worst day for the men in black and gold. Every one-a-day is. It may seem illogical that a day with only one practice can be worse than a day with two. But the one-a-day 3 p.m. broiler is much hotter than the two-a-day morning and night sessions. And with only one practice, the day is chocked full of long, dull meetings.

The first item of business on this one-a-day is weight lifting. This is the domain of the strength and conditioning coaches. They are two sharply cut blocks of marble who played football at the college level and competed nationally in power lifting. They are men's men, genuine, no-frills, stand-up guys. The head man is Rock Gullickson, and the assistant is the bald-domed Evan Marcus, but they might as well be called "Rock and Stone."

Rock and Stone are thrilled that the Saints are actually lifting during training camp. Many head coaches don't provide the time for it. But Haslett allows a 30-40 minute weight training session on the morning of every one-a-day. During that time, the players squeeze in five to seven exercises, doing three to five sets of five to eight reps of each. "It's pretty intense," says Rock. "It's designed to maintain their strength during this period. It's not designed to take anything away from practice. You know you hate to have a guy go into practice and say, 'I'm tired from weight training.'"

There's no need to do the extra speed, agility, and conditioning work the players must do in the off-season because as Stone puts it, "Everything they do right now (in practice) is speed, agility, and conditioning."

Conditioning the rookies to NFL weight lifting is one of the toughest parts of the strength coaches' jobs. "They've all got a long way to go," says Rock. Nonetheless, the coaches have been pleased with the undrafted rookies' work ethic. They point to the enthusiasm of Jamal Brooks, "great attitude to do extra all the time" and to the push of Pete Destefano, "he's competitive."

The weight room can be as competitive as the practice field, even though the competition is more internal. My request to Rock and Stone to observe some of this competitiveness during this morning's session was denied by Haslett. Haslett must be worried about me putting a *gris-gris* on one of his players. He's petrified that my evil eye will temporarily zap the player of his strength so that a big weight falls on his toe and ends his season.

～

At noon, tight end Cam Cleeland and wide receivers P.J. Franklin and L.C. Stevens are walking into the cafeteria. They are moving as if they are sloshing through snow in galoshes. Cleeland tells them, "If I took a week off, I'd still be tired." He has good reason to be exhausted. Last week, he battled the flu and went under the needle for dehydration treatment.

Stevens turns to Cleeland and says, "I started camp off at 220, now I'm at 210."

At the 3 p.m. practice, the pounds continue to shed as the temperatures rise for another liquid scorcher. When the horn blows, special teams coach Al Everest shouts, "I think I can. I think I can."

Everest has a saying he often tells players during particularly torrid practices. "It's hot, all right," he says. "So we know it's hot. You know it's hot. Everybody knows it's hot. But, to me, real heat is sitting in your house and not being able to pay the bills to cool it down. That's heat."

Psychological perceptions aside, the heat out here is real enough. And perhaps it's the reality of the oppressive conditions that have squelched every potential fight thus far in camp. It's as if two players tangle, start pushing, then they just stop. But this afternoon, they aren't stopping. Offensive guard Justin Burroughs and defensive tackle Winfield Garnett are going at it. Garnett is one large human. He's listed at 6-6, 305, but he might as well be a walking oak tree. He is getting the better of the smaller Burroughs. The scuffle turns WWF when Garnett hip-tosses Burroughs. Then, teammates quickly intercede, with Chase Raynock pulling away Garnett.

Later in one-on-ones, Chase the peacemaker takes down an off-balance Garnett. Next, Desmond Gibson swims Jason McEndoo, then Robert Brannon steamrolls Jay Hagood. Chalk one up for the undrafted rookies.

～

Wednesday, July 26, 2000, 8:50 p.m.

Something is lurking beneath the lights of Guidry Stadium. Pete Destefano can sense it. He's back there in the deep middle, thinking run. It's 9-on-7, and 9-on-7 is usually about run, supporting the run, stopping the run. Since Pete made his big pick two nights ago, things have been strange. He finds that Coach Venturi is constantly mentioning his competitor Eric Johnson's name in meetings. Pete thought the gap between him and Johnson was widening, but apparently

him, "The press box is full."

"What? Full?" I say. "It's a preseason game."

"It's the largest media market in the country."

"Still, it's a preseason game. We're not talking the Super Bowl, here. There can't be that many requests."

"It's full," he says.

"But I made my request at the same time as the other guys. How do they decide who gets a credential and who doesn't? I mean, how do they kick mine aside and pick theirs?"

"Uh, radio, newspaper, and TV get credentialed first."

"Well, you know I've already bought my plane ticket. It's nonrefundable."

"The press box is full."

"I guess I'll have to buy a ticket and sit in the stands."

I walk away relieved that I haven't lost my cool. I've already gotten into an argument once this week with this same media policeman. He told me on Monday that I could no longer wait for the players in the long air-conditioned corridor that leads to the entrance to the dining room. Haslett and his police force had allowed the media to wait there last week, then decided on Monday that we would wait outside in the heat. In my part of the country, which happens to be this part of the country, we call this impolite. We call it a lack of common courtesy to have our guests waiting outside, squinting in the sun, after they've already sweat the salt out of their skin while sitting through a two-and-a-half hour practice.

Considering all that's happened, I'm not surprised that the media police appear to be trying to keep me out of the Meadowlands. But I am a little mystified at how stupid they think I am. They don't realize that I've already telephoned Sharon with the Jets' media relations department. Sharon told me the Jets never even received my request. She said that if a visiting team like the Saints put in a request, they automatically issue the credential. They don't sit there and scrutinize it.

Pulling out my cell phone at practice, I call Sharon to see if the credential request that I've made through the Jets has been confirmed by her boss. Sharon tells me they've issued me the credential. She will later tell me that the press box was never full, never even close. At game time, the mammoth 400-seat press box that sits high above

Giants Stadium will be less than half full. There will be way too many empty seats to even thinking about counting them.

~

Later in practice, Chase Raynock is listening to the count in one-on-one drills. He's *tête-à-tête* with Darren Howard. When the ball snaps, the rookie bonus baby fires into him, and Chase almost immediately takes him down. On the second go-round, Howard does no better, and out of frustration, initiates a brief tussle, which he quickly abandons.

"All I got to say about that," says Chase after practice, "is he came up to me the first time, and I put him down on the ground, and I smacked him down. And he told me, he lined up across from me and said, 'I'm coming right through your ass this time.' I go, 'Bring it on then.' And he come up through, and he tried to go up inside me so I just took him and turned him over the top. I mean it should have been left at that. He got a little rowdy down underneath there, but it wasn't too big. You just gotta do what you gotta do."

Despite being the Mueller-Haslett era's first big selection, Darren Howard hasn't been overly impressive. He's a sleek and athletic 6-3, 281, a real combine special. He doesn't, though, have much of a motor. As any scout will tell you, a high-horsepower motor is essential for any d-lineman. As d-line coach Sam Clancy says, linemen must be "high intensity" guys with a "quick twitch." The label placed on Howard coming out of Kansas State was that, despite having a productive career, he didn't always maintain his intensity level. So considering his reputation, it's a little puzzling why the Saints used their first pick to take him, much less make him an automatic starter.

"He's still young, you know," says Chase. "He ain't got as much pressure, you know. They're handing him his stuff. He gets a little pressure on him saying he's not playing, I guarantee you he's gonna pick it up."

Things have picked up for Chase this week. He's sleeping better thanks to Coop loaning him a few team-issued sleeping pills. And today, he's received some help in an unexpected, unpleasant way. Fellow offensive guard Justin Burroughs quit the team today, saying his heart was no longer into playing football.

"He was doing a good job," says Chase. "You put a year and a half into it (like Burroughs did). You put that much time into it. You're almost there. I mean, he's doing good. And coach said he's doing a good job and stuff, and then you're gonna quit? Man, that don't make no sense to me. You been working all this time for this, and you're gonna quit? That's just ridiculous.

"If someone's gonna give me a million, two million, three million, even two hundred thousand to play football this year, shoot, I'll take that, and I'll run. That's a sucker deal right there."

Chase admits that Burroughs did him a favor by quitting. "There was a little bit of relief," he says. "You'll sit there, and you'll watch film, and you try to do the mental cuts in your head sometimes." He doesn't buy the talk from players who say they're only competing against themselves. "That's bullshit. I guarantee everyone who's fighting for a spot on this team is doing the mental cuts, who's doing what and doing how on the team. They take a look at that, and say, 'Did I do better than him today? How's that mark for me and stuff,' you know?"

He'll know more about how he stands come game time. "I want to compete against guys who are not going to know what's going on all the time, you know, who are not going to know what the plays and stuff are," he says. "I'm going out there to win. I'm not going out there to be somebody's slapdick pushover."

However, the odds are Chase won't be out there often. "He's not gonna get a lot of playing time," says his position coach, Jack Henry.

While Chase Raynock probably won't play much, most of his fellow undrafted rookies will be on the field long enough to make an impression. They know the apple they're about to bite is a big one. It's not just game one NFL, it's New York. It's the market of all markets, the city of all cities. It's 100-floor skyscrapers, and 16-lane expressways. It's the legacy of the Babe and Broadway Joe. It's the *Times*, the *Daily News*, the *Post*, the *Voice*, the *Star-Ledger*, *Newsday*, WCBS, WNBC, WABC, and dozens of other W-thises and W-thats. It's *New York City*.

/ TEN /

JETS

Friday, July 28, 2000, 12:00 P.M.

Look at this craziness. Sane people are moving insanely. In droves, in piles, pushing, scooting, people, millions of them on one freaking sidewalk. The pace is so fleet, the atmosphere is so chaotic. One minute, you're crawling in Thibodaux, just yawning away. The next you're in midtown Manhattan, and you're damn near running, and you still can't walk with them. There are all kinds of cultures and colors and clothes, alike only in their ability to move with the pack without breaking stride. You slip into a deli, and the workers back there are slicing tomatoes so fast they're about to chop off their fingers. They don't seem to care. You grab your lox bagel, and you try to go outside, but you are swimming upstream. You realize that you may have run with the bulls in Pamplona, but that was nothing compared to this. This is New York. This is insanity.

~

On Saturday night at Giants Stadium, it's New York on warp speed. It's missiles flying. It's Air Force jets diving and crossing and human Jets bashing and crashing. They're so blurry you can't see them. Ask Desmond Gibson. With the first quarter not yet elapsed, Desmond finds himself on the line of scrimmage, staring at first team "Gang Green." He's hearing Vinny Testaverde bark out signals. He's watching his Pittsburgh homeboy Curtis Martin get into his stance. He's nose to nose with Pro Bowl center Kevin Mawae. The first play is a pass play. He knows that much. The rest is all hazy green and white.

The second play snaps, and the Pro Bowl is under him. In a nanosecond, Mawae is clawing ahold of Desmond like a wampus cat, pushing him aside, opening the middle.

After these two plays, Desmond adjusts, but never gets used to what he calls "the speed and power of the NFL."

To a man, the undrafted rookies are awestruck. The pace is so much more rapid than in practice, so much swifter than the scrimmage. Their bodies can hardly stand the rush.

"I had so much adrenaline I felt like I was gonna pass out," says Pete Destefano. "I was floating. Felt so fast, so quick."

The first half quickly destroys the Saints. Three starters go down with injuries. Two, tight-end Cam Cleeland and cornerback Steve Israel are out for the season. Safety Rob Kelly will be lost for 6-8 weeks. The Saints lose the field battle, too. One Jet is beating the Saints' defense almost by himself. Wide receiver Wayne Chrebet, a former undrafted rookie, makes catch after catch, including a 75-yard touchdown. Chrebet is a Jersey gym rat who grew up 10 minutes from this stadium. He walked-on at little Hofstra, then walked-on to the Jets, who happen to train at Hofstra. He's now one of the most dependable receivers in the league and a local folk hero as chronicled in his book, *Every Down, Every Distance* (Doubleday, 1999).

Inspired by Chrebet's story, the Saints' undrafted rookies wait patiently on the sidelines. Pete Destefano and Jamal Brooks won't take their helmets off, even when the Saints' offense is on the field. "You can't be intense just sitting there, hoping," says Jamal. "It's like waiting for a baby. You'd be in labor for 30 hours. The first hour you're real hyper, but around the 20th hour, you just like, 'When (is it) gonna happen?'"

It happens for Jamal with 6:28 to go in the second quarter. He's not in for long. He, like most of the undrafted rookies, doesn't play much until the second half. In the fourth quarter, Jamal makes a nice stop on a screen, limiting the gain to one yard.

On the same series, Pete makes a touchdown-saving, open-field tackle. Pete, though, is shocked by what happened before he ever got in the game. "Somehow, I lost my spot in the last day or so," he says.

Without telling him, the coaches moved Eric Johnson ahead of him at free safety. Pete didn't know of the change until Johnson was sent into the game with the third team. Pete was forced to watch Johnson play two full series before he subbed in for him on the third.

"I decided as soon as it happened that I wasn't going to dwell on it and tried not to be negative," says Pete. "I didn't want to be negative going in there. I figured I'd just get that out of my head and worry about myself."

The head-clearing began in pregame for the Saints' rookie kicking duo, Shayne Graham and Bill LaFleur. What was a warm-up for everyone else was showtime for them. High up in the press box, scouts were taking notes on their every swing of the leg. They came from 18 NFL teams and 2 CFL teams, and they timed the hang time and noted the distances on every punt and kickoff and recorded the accuracy of Shayne's field goals. A full cadre of scouts like this one is commonplace during preseason when teams are trimming rosters and releasing players that become eligible to be claimed by other teams. While Shayne and Bill would prefer to stick with the Saints, they know the game.

During the actual game, Bill has a solid, but unspectacular punting performance. Shayne nails his lone extra point attempt but doesn't fare as well on his two kickoffs, which only travel to the 12- and 14-yard lines. He also watches in empathy as Doug Brien misses a key field goal. "I've been there, too. I've seen them go wide left, and I've seen them go wide right. Nobody makes 'em all."

After the game in the locker room, the Saints' four-point loss is an afterthought. Coach Haslett is visibly disturbed over losing his three starters, especially Cleeland, who looked in camp like the Saints' biggest offensive weapon. With a torn left Achilles tendon, Cleeland's powerful 270-pound body and remarkably nimble feet will now be of no use to the team. The Mueller-Haslett honeymoon has officially ended. Any more optimism will be colored by the reality of all that has happened tonight.

The undrafted rookies are a bit dismayed by the whole scene. They're still reeling from the blitzkrieg. Bedazzled Robert Brannon, who assisted on a tackle for a loss, is so hoarse from yelling he's croaking like a frog. When asked how it felt to run out on the field, he croaks, "I don't know. I can't explain it right now."

Pete Destefano is having a difficult time explaining what's happened. First, starting free safety Rob Kelly goes down with a fractured lower leg, meaning Pete moves from third team to second. Then, second team safety Darren Perry plays horribly, blowing his coverage on the long touchdown pass to Chrebet. Suddenly, it looks as if Pete has a real chance to compete for the starting job. Just as Pete's hopes start rising, in midgame he learns that Eric Johnson has been moved ahead of him. He runs it all through his head, takes a breath, then looks me right in the eye.

"I'm telling you this, Woody," he says. "I'm gonna be a starter. I'm gonna be a starter this year. If I get on this team, I'll be a starter."

Over in the next row of lockers, Chase Raynock is red-faced. Steam is rising off his head. He is letting out a string of curse words. I try to talk to him about his excellent offensive pass blocking on the only series he played. He responds, "I don't wanna fuckin' sit on the sideline and not play. I came here to play, man. I didn't want to sit on the sideline." He first entered the game for an offensive series with only 1:12 left on the clock.

"You mad because you didn't play earlier?"

"Fuck yeah, I'm mad. I didn't fucking come out here to sit. They didn't give me a chance to see what I can do."

"Let's go back. I know you're mad right now, but let's go back to before the game. What was it like? Were you nervous at all? Were you pumped?"

"I was ready to play. I came out ready to play tonight. I wanted to play. That's what I came here to do. I came here to play football."

Still fuming, Chase lumbers off toward the team buses. I now realize that I misjudged him. I shouldn't have sized him up as too soft to play at this level. Contrarily, he's got so much fire inside him he might burn down the stadium. While he may not be reacting to this setback in the most mature, professional manner, his response is proper, very proper.

On the plane ride home, there will be a lot to stew over for our eight heroes. They may not realize just how New York City has put their opportunity in perspective. It would have been difficult for them to know this, being that they were forced to stay holed up in their hotel in Newark all day, looking out the window at the cesspools and tank farms. Had they been across the Hudson River, way atop the World Trade Center, they could've seen a sea of cities and states, of architecture and islands. Depending on the clarity of the day, the eye may pick up territory holding 14 million people. And less than one one-thousandth of one percent of those people have ever had the chance to play in the National Football League.

Most of the rest of them are working themselves into daily exhaustion for a salary that is at least five times less than the NFL rookie minimum of $193,000. One Manhattan resident, a lawyer friend of mine, works every day from 9 a.m. to 11 p.m. and eats breakfast, lunch, and dinner at his desk. He makes good money, but he doesn't make close to $193K. He will, one day, but he's been practicing law at top-notch firms for five years, has a law degree from NYU, and he hasn't made it yet. An NFL football player may work hard, but he doesn't work that hard. He only has to endure a training camp schedule for a month, not year-round.

So as the Saints ride home on a direct-chartered flight, taking in a premium movie, eating premium food, their undrafted rookies don't mind sitting bunched up next to each other while the older heads get an empty seat in between them. Each knows that he'll have to perform better than he did tonight. He'll have to be better than the average rookie. He'll have to show that he's worthy of every penny of what might become his first $12,000 game check.

~

Monday, July 31, 2000, 5:00 p.m.

Randy Mueller has pulled his hair trigger again. He's just left the land of Wall Street, but he's still there in spirit. "I think you've got to be able to react on the run," he says. "Boom, boom, boom, as things come up." Today, he's booming. The Saints have traded linebacker K.D. Williams and the team's third round pick in 2001 to the Green Bay Packers for quarterback Aaron Brooks and tight end Lamont Hall.

The Saints have released running back Dino Philyaw, of whom Coach Haslett said in the final minicamp, "Dino does a great job running routes. We don't have a linebacker who can cover him. He's just got to stay healthy." In the end, Dino apparently needed more than a clean bill of health. The Saints also released quarterback Pat Barnes, which means his performance at Rox's Bar will be his last.

These transactions certainly won't be Mueller's last ones. He's spent the off-season making more moves than a Bourbon Street break-dancer. When the free agent signing period began on February 11, 2000, the contracts started flying in Saintsville. It became a game of nonstop, real-life fantasy football. Over the next three months, Mueller signed an unprecedented 12 veteran free agents formerly of other teams and spent more than $20 million in signing bonuses. He traded away the old Saints not to his liking, and cut the ones that he couldn't trade.

With each trigger pull, Mueller was in the process of completely making over the franchise. Fifty-six percent of the players who began training camp had never before worn a Saints' uniform. In addition to the new older heads, Mueller brought in players from the Canadian league, from NFL Europe, nine draft picks, and eleven (now eight) rookie free agents with no professional football experience.

Signing the rookie free agents was a rush for Mueller. It always has been. He says the process has come a long way. "When I was in Seattle, we had 30 guys who we employed around the country, not people who worked for us, but car salesmen, all kinds of people. We used to send them out all over the country with contracts, armed with contracts. They would go to the kid's house, and they would kind of corner them off to the side, make sure he didn't get drafted and sign him."

Mueller says this hotbox-recruiting technique has ended within the last five years. The postdraft signings are now handled over the phone with the players' agents. But as fast as things were done with the car salesmen, et al., they're much faster now. The teams use every man available, the GM, other front office personnel, scouts, coaches, to call the players or their agents as the draft begins to wind down. Then the contracts are quickly banged out between the agents and the administrators.

"Really, that's when you act spontaneously in that, after the draft, an hour later, all these guys are done. It's all signed and done, an hour, an hour and a half later," says Mueller. "Agents know that the rosters fill up quickly so they have to make a deal quickly. Yeah, it's boom, boom, boom, boom, boom. It's kind of a contest internally to see who can get the most guys committed quickly."

Football has been a serious contest for Mueller since he was a kid.

While his apparently soft, even slouched physique may not appear to be that of an ex-athlete, Mueller was in fact an Honorable Mention Little All-America quarterback at Linfield College in Oregon. As a senior, he led Linfield to the 1982 NAIA Division II National Championship.

After graduation, Mueller took a pro personnel assistant's job with the Seattle Seahawks, a team that he had worked for on and off since he was a teenaged ball boy. Until he joined the Saints this year, the Seahawks have been his only full-time employer.

Only 39, Mueller feels fortunate to have the keys to an NFL franchise. Despite his premature gray hair, his face is cherubic enough to show his youth. Nevertheless, he comes across as savvy and confident, yet not arrogant. He's small-town friendly, coming by it naturally after growing up in tiny St. Maries, Idaho.

In his Pacific Northwest accent, he talks of how he manages the personnel decisions that will bring a roster of 87 players down to a final one of 53. "It's not a one-man job. It's not just me. It's not just me and Jim (Haslett). It's Rick (Mueller, Randy's brother and Director of Player Personnel). It's Mickey (Loomis, Director of Football Administration). It's Charles (Bailey, Assistant General Manager). It's the scouts. We meet every day. We talk about everything all the time."

Mueller conducts a personnel meeting in the morning before practice and in the evening after practice. For these first two and a half weeks of camp, he sends his scouts to practice every day. For a particular practice, each scout has certain players and/or positions that they will review. Unlike some other general managers, Mueller attends every practice personally, and most of the time he has a definite agenda. It's clear that while Haslett and the others have their opinions, ultimately, the buck stops with Mueller.

If a long shot has any shot of making this team, he better impress Randy Mueller, and if it hasn't happened already, it better begin tomorrow, during the Saints' two practices in Jacksonville against the Jaguars. If it doesn't happen sooner instead of later, the amiable man in charge won't hesitate to make a very nonamiable maneuver.

~

Tuesday, August 1, 2000, 8:00 a.m.

At the moment, the Jamal juice isn't gushing. The spring, the pep, all that trademark free-flowing elixir just ain't swishing this morning. Jamal Brooks is standing on one of three 100-yard verdant putting greens that are the Jacksonville Jaguars practice fields. He's waiting for someone to say, "Hut," waiting to cover the Jaguar running back, but he might as well be standing in a grocery line. He's sinking into the mattress-like surface, made softer by the glistening dew. When the ball snaps, he's already behind.

The Jag runs, cuts, catches. Jamal isn't close.

"Finish!" yells coach John Bunting, who seems as linebacker intense as he was during his playing days for the Philadelphia Eagles. "Make the tackle, Jamal. Come on. Let's go!"

Jamal is having a hard time going. In one week's time, he will have gone from Thibodaux to Newark to Thibodaux to Jacksonville to Thibodaux to Minneapolis and back to Thibodaux. "I mean, as soon as you finally get used to your room, now you're out of your room," says Jamal. But today has got to be the worst. The plane arrived last night at midnight. Then, at 5:45 a.m. eastern time, the alarm clock rings. But Jamal's on central time so he really rose at 4:45. He really started practice at 7 a.m. "This is the NFL," he says. "You just got to suck it up and do it."

But this morning, Jamal is not doing it. Later, the head man himself jumps the rook for missing an assignment on a passing play. Jamal tries to shake it all away. He tries to brush off the pain of his hyper-extended right middle finger, which he wears in a splint when he's not playing. He tries to forget that the coaches didn't move him up to second team when they traded K.D. Williams yesterday. He thinks he should be the second-teamer and not Phil Ward, but he's trying not to dwell on it. He's trying not to dwell in one place, period. He's doing his best just to get off the ground and get back that good ol' Jamal juice.

Jamal isn't the only one plodding. All of the Saints seem to be a step behind. It isn't helping that they're practicing against the Jaguars, who were 14-2 last year and have been to two of the last four AFC Championship games. Everything about the Jags seems different than what the boys in black and gold are used to seeing, used to doing.

For starters, it's all here. The training camp, the practice facility, the administrative offices, and the Sunday stage are all right here, inside and next to ALLTEL Stadium. The Jags never have to leave. No other franchise has done it quite like this, hiring the head coach one year before the inaugural 1995 season, building a brand-new stadium just in time for the first game, then after the first year of losing, reeling off four straight winning seasons. The whole operation reeks of cleanliness and efficiency.

In warm-ups, the Jaguars' stretching is perfectly synchronized, like a mass water ballet. Their drills are so precise it's as if they were choreographed. Presiding over it all are the beady blue eyes of head coach Tom Coughlin. Coughlin's detailed plan keeps practice humming. As up-tempo as the Saints' practices are, the Jags move from play to play and from drill to drill even faster.

"It's just go, go get it done," says Chase Raynock.

"It's faster because they don't take time to adjust," says D.J. Cooper. "If you mess up on a play, they go to the next play 'cause one of my friends that's on the team, Emmanuel Smith, he said the coach preaches that you don't get the playback in a game. So they don't repeat stuff, so that's the way their tempo is faster."

"I like it so much better," says Pete Destefano. "I bet you'll ask anybody. It was so much better."

It's true. They all like it better. The one-and-a-half-hour practice will pass before they know it.

"I like that a lot more than staying out there two and a half hours," says Chase, "you know after awhile things start to drag out there (in a typical Saints' practice)."

But there's no drag with the Jag. Everything clicks. "Fuck, they're a good team," says Pete. It's an odd feeling for Pete, being back there in the deep middle, staring at Mark Brunell under center, at Jimmy Smith and Keenan McCardell on the flanks. This time, it's not speed that floors him.

"The precision between the quarterback and receivers was a night and day difference," he says. "I mean when they turn around, the ball is there. I mean the balls are almost perfectly thrown every time. I'm not saying that Jeff (Blake) doesn't throw a good ball—he does. But I think he hasn't been around his receivers as long. There's not like that connection."

It doesn't take long for reality to connect with Coop when he twists his already nagging left ankle, and it finally forces him off the practice field. "I'm gonna get treatment on it every day now," he says. "I've been noticing my game decreasing because of it. I can't cut, you know, just do stuff on a pass rush that I usually would do."

For Coop and his teammates, lunch is at the swank Radisson Hotel, where the Jaguars bed and board for camp. Its five-story, plant-covered atrium doesn't bear even the slightest resemblance to the dated lobby of Ellender Dormitory. The meal is fancy Chinese food with lots of pastas and rice and an ultrafresh salad. After the players' repast, they struggle back toward the team buses. Chase says his legs are a "little bit out from under him right now."

"I'm tired. I'm exhausted. I'm tired," says Pete. "It's almost like you get so tired that your body starts waking up again where you kinda get that extra little pep, and that's where I am right now. But when this wears off by tonight, I'm gonna be drained."

As Pete walks off, he seems drained right now. He hits the buses with the other players, and as they take their seats, they almost immediately pass out. Their heads fall against the window, against the seat cushion, into the crack in between. Robert Brannon's big baby face is rising and falling to a sleepy beat.

$$\sim$$

At the opening of the afternoon practice, something is different. The Saints have acclimated. They are flying around, doing their best to be aggressive in what is another nontackle practice. And once again, Jamal has the juice. He goes one-on-one in pass coverage with Fred Taylor, the Jaguars' best running back, and locks right on him, denies him the ball. He is bouncing around again, letting the Jamal juice whiz through his veins, pushing him past this morning's dreadful practice and into only the present and the future.

The future is much easier for him than the past. He won't tell you that, though. He'll talk about the good memories of days gone by. Growing up in South Central Los Angeles, being raised by a single parent, needing roommates to help pay the rent, being surrounded by Cripps and Bloods—these don't seem like the best of circumstances. But he'll only say, "It was some tough times, but you can live in suburbia and have tough times."

The tough times are literally marked on him. He has several keloid scars on his torso. But when you ask him, "How'd you get those keloids?"

He responds, "Oh, football, and rough little life down in L.A., just some little personal things."

"Were you in a knife fight or something?"

"Oh no, just being young and dumb, basically. I don't really talk about those much. It's just being young and dumb."

He won't talk about those scars because they are negatives, and there's nothing in his makeup that's negative. He is positive about anything, everything. He won't dampen his mood or put a derogatory spin of any kind on what he's doing right now. He's not gonna make excuses, not gonna mention poverty, race, lack of great size, lack of great speed, being from a small college, or being undrafted. He feels too blessed to have this chance to talk himself out of succeeding at it. He's all about staying up, drinking the natural elixir. Keloids, setbacks, coaches yelling, the Jamal juice just washes over them all.

~

During the afternoon session, an Atlantic breeze washes over the field. "It's cooler down here. That's for sure," says Desmond Gibson.

The milder climate and the nouveau riche trappings will soon end for the Saints. Tonight, they'll be leaving the country club and heading for the cane field. They'll be moving away from the artificial and immersing themselves in the pastoral. Their takeoff from Jacksonville will be delayed three hours, but the real inconveniences won't come until tomorrow.

/ ELEVEN /

TICKLE YOU PURPLE

WEDNESDAY, AUGUST 2, 2000, 12:00 P.M.

This may be the rain out the players are craving. The sky is graying; the clouds are starting to move faster. The players know that if the rain forces them into the Houma-Terrebonne Civic Center, it can't be that tough. They know how injury-conscious their coach is, especially since the Jets game. He can only make them go so hard indoors on the turf. And how bad can it be in the air-conditioning? Maybe Haslett will just scratch his blonde hair and throw his hands in the air. This may be the day he gives them the afternoon off.

Chase Raynock walks out of the cafeteria, looks up at all the gray and squints as if he's looking into a Rocky Mountain sun. He's asked if he wants it to rain. He hesitates. He knows the older heads are around. He doesn't want to give the wrong answer. "It doesn't matter," he says. "We still gotta practice anyway."

Willie Roaf hears this and says loudly, "Come on, rain. Come on, rain. Come on, rain!"

The rain never comes. At 3 p.m., it's practice as usual.

"In the huddle, in the huddle, in the huddle," yells Zook.

"Let's go. Get in the huddle," barks out another coach.

"Huddle, huddle," screams a third.

"Fuck, get in the huddle," shouts a fourth.

The instruction to huddle is incessant. The coaches make the command even though the players are making a beeline for the huddle.

It's as if, when a play is blown dead, a player is under the impression he can head over to the shade of the oak tree and take a nap. It's like if no one tells a player to huddle, he'll hightail it back to the dorm and challenge the housemother to a game of Ping-Pong.

Zook regurgitates, "In the huddle, in the huddle, in the huddle."

Pete Destefano would rather not hear this today, especially not from Zook. While waiting for the fourth team to be called, Pete is taking a knee, with his helmet off. He never does this. It's permitted, but it's just not something he does. At the moment, he's had it. He doesn't understand how the starter at his position can go down with an injury, and the result is he gets less reps. At least, he thought he would maintain his third slot, even though Eric Johnson was moved ahead of him in the Jets game. Instead, they've moved Shannon Garrett over from cornerback to second-team safety. They're giving him extra reps to get acquainted with the position. Pete's the one getting squeezed.

He thinks it came down to one play; that dreaded play action during the 9-on-7 under the lights. He can't believe it. He gets penalized for a chickenshit drill, but Darren Perry gives up a touchdown in the game, and he gets promoted. Pete says he's been told that the coaches know he's talented, but it's more of a "trust thing." "They want to be able to trust that when I go in there I'm not gonna be able to fuck up a big play," says Pete.

He wonders, though, how the coaches can find out what he has unless they play him, unless they give him his reps. Venturi's answer to that: "I always say life is not fair in the National Football League." Damn right it's not, Pete thinks. It's also not fair, he thinks, for Zook and Venturi to jump his shit when he makes a mistake, but make an excuse for the older heads and the drafted guys when they screw up. Draft pick Michael Hawthorne gets beat deep in the scrimmage, and he loses nothing. Pete gets sucked in on a traditional run drill, and he gets cast aside. It doesn't make sense. None of it. Zook and Venturi have got him afraid to make a mistake. He's not thinking alleys and blowups anymore. He's just thinking and thinking.

He remembers Jacksonville. He remembers how calm the coaches were when their players made a mistake. But then when he makes his mistake in J-ville, it's a different deal altogether. He remembers looking at Zook for the defensive call, not realizing that the coaches aren't going to give a signal. He knows the mistake is his mistake. He should've made the call himself. But the reaction, Jesus, the reaction. Zook loses it. Zook tells him, "You're just a fuckup."

How do you respond to that? You're 24 years old, confident as a crocodile, yet fragile as a figurine and your coach calls you a fuckup. Maybe it was a slip. Maybe, it was heat-of-battle Zook, who's just as likely to compliment as he is to criticize. Maybe, probably, it wasn't personal. So what, Pete thinks. He said it. "You're just a fuckup." What kind of psychology is that?

He looks over at Haslett, loping around the huddle. He likes him. Haslett is consistent. His blowups are rare, but equal. He tells rookie Austin Wheatley, "Catch the fucking ball." He also tells the 10-year-older head Jake Reed, "Catch the fucking ball." It's not that they don't know to catch it. They certainly aren't dropping them on purpose. Reed's position is wide "receiver," not a wide "dropper." Nonetheless, coaches will yell out of exasperation, and Pete's point is Haslett's yelling is nondiscriminatory. Consistency, he can respect that.

He can't respect Zook, though. Can't. Doesn't want to hear him today at all. It's all so damn frustrating. They put him back there in the deep middle or the deep half, and they rarely throw his way. It's that Saints' West Coast offense, full of short routes and dump-offs. The bombs are few and far between. When it comes to run drills, they won't let you tackle. It's so damn nonphysical here, the most nonphysical camp he's ever been in. They say that's what the games are for, but you've got to get in there and get your rhythm. You've got to have more chances to make more tackles. You've got to ring 'em up. It takes reps to do that, series after series of reps. He needs this Vikings game. He knows he's got to clear away the crap. The hell with Zook. Just let me play, he thinks. Just let me play.

~

Over on the offensive line, Chase Raynock knows that he's going to play. Attrition deems that he must. He's been running second team all day, and he's ready. Bring on the "Purple People Eaters," he says inwardly. Outwardly, his position coach says, "I mean he'll fight his butt off. I don't have any question about that." Yes, he will fight. He'll show 'em that they made a mistake in that Jets game. He's no "slapdick pushover." The boys in purple will find that out, so will the coaches in black and gold.

~

Thursday, August 3, 2000, 11:00 a.m.

The grassy stage is a flutter and a clutter with activity. It's gridiron Ice Capades. Legs are churning up the field, down the field. Bodies are moving in from the sideline, out toward the sideline. Huddles are formed, then broken. Balls are kicked, then caught. It's mass, chaotic choreography. And in the middle of it all, not visible at the moment, buried among all the oversized dancers, is the choreographer, Dr. Al Everest. He is belting out instructions to his special teams units in his raspy, cigarette-influenced voice, which is always on the verge of getting hoarse, probably more from the need to shout than the need for nicotine.

From behind the yellow rope, there is no way to decipher what he's saying. Even on the field, even when the words are clear, their meaning may escape the unlettered rookie. "He speak his own language out there," says Coop. "'One versus two plus.' You know, what is that? I don't know what 'two plus' is. He'll say that, and he expect us to already know."

Everest's expectations must be great. He has to prepare each special teams unit four deep. Four kick coverage teams, four kick return, four field goal, etc., etc., and he only has so much time. It's not an easy thing to do, he says, in fact, "it's almost impossible." But it must be done and done now because this is preseason.

"The objective of preseason to me is to number one, make sure you keep the best players," he says. "And the only way you're gonna find out who the best player is, is to play him."

So every day he plays the ones who just might have the ability to make it work. "We're looking for a number of things," he says. "One is attitude about it, respect for the position. Two, you look for some instincts, a guy that can make plays in spades. And then there's two kinds of guys. One is just a great athlete that has a chance to make things happen on his own. And the other one is a damn good athlete that's gotta learn how to do it, and he's gotta be focused and he's really gotta stay after the job to get it done. And the final thing is you're looking at size of the guys. I mean, you can't have 12 DBs (on the final roster). You can't have 15 linebackers."

In the final analysis, except for the kicker, punter, and long snapper, his special-teamers can't be *just* special-teamers. First, they must excel on defense or offense. But if they're not an offensive or defensive starter, they must be able to play special teams and play it well. And for a long shot, proving himself as a special teams standout is tantamount. "There's always some borderline decisions," says Everest, "where like Jim (Haslett) says, 'Who do you like out of these three guys? Who can help us win games out of these three guys? They're all about the same cornerback or the same safety or the same level linebacker.'" In these cases, the decision will come down to special teams, and the most "special" player will win.

It takes a special coach to do this job. The margins of error are narrower. The need to motivate is greater. The teaching is the most diverse because it includes an offensive component on the return teams, defense on the coverage teams, and high specialization for the kicker and the punter. It's high-speed blocking. It's higher-speed tackling. It's precision under fire. The coach must have the background to handle it all.

When it comes to background, Everest certainly has one that jumps right out of the media guide. Few coaches in the NFL have written doctoral dissertations, much less coached teams like the Legnano Frogs and the Pesaro Angels in the football hotbed that borders the Ligurian and Adriatic Seas. Everest has taught football at levels that range from high school to college to the Italian League to the Pro Spring Football League to the Arena Football League to the Canadian Football League to finally in 1996, the Arizona Cardinals of the National Football League. Along the way, he was the athletic director of the American School Foundation in Mexico City and a head baseball coach for seven years at U.S. International University, where he also picked up his doctorate in education.

With all that globetrotting, Everest fits comfortably in the multifaceted, helter-skelter world of special teams. He has seen so many cultures and so many places that he finds an analogy to suit each situation. For instance, he compares blocking in the return game to trapping monkeys. "In Africa, they've caught monkeys for thousands of years by digging a hole and putting fruit in a hole. And (the monkey) would go in there, and the monkey would grab the fruit, and when he made the fist, he couldn't get his hand back out of the hole. So they (the hunters) walk up to him, he's screaming and hollering. They hit him on the head with a stick."

If the monkey had just unclenched his fist and let the fruit go, he could have slipped his hand right out of the hole. By the same token, "if you lose your block on a kickoff return or a punt return, don't chase him 'cause now you're part of the kickoff coverage. Let the fruit go and go get the next level. Don't be a monkey on the field. Make good decisions. Know what your alternatives are when you get beat."

Everest has many alternatives when it comes to pumping up his players. He throws out sayings like he's a paperboy flinging the daily news. "Anybody who gave his best never regretted it." "Nothing great was accomplished without enthusiasm." Or the frequent, "Ball 'til you fall!" No matter what the message is, Everest says a person's motivation must come from the right source.

"People in the public think that because they make money, that's motivation. Money is probably, after you get it, the worst form of motivation there is. The number one form of motivation is to be the best at what you do, no matter what it is. And then second is earned income which reflects your commitment to your job, and third is not letting down people who are counting on you."

Everest is counting on the preseason to reveal some quality special teams players. During the Jets game, none of the eight undrafted really made their mark on special teams. They will have to elevate their performances come Saturday. There are only so many opportunities to look like a pigskin gorilla (and not his monkey cousin).

～

Saturday, August 5, 2000, 10:30 a.m.

The players are trapped. Downtown Minneapolis is all around them, but they're confined to the Marriott City Center. They have been since their arrival last night. At present, they're in a meeting. They seem to meet more than legislators. While this meeting will be a short one, the coaches basically own them during game weekends. Nevertheless, many are happy to chill out in their rooms and catch up on sleep. "I just get a movie," says Jamal Brooks. "Me and my roommate (Joe Tuipala) watch a movie and just laugh, talk, and enjoy the time we get to just relax. During the week, it's here, there, here, there, here, there, meetings, practice, meetings, practice, eating, practice, meetings."

It may be necessary for Jamal and his teammates to simply relax and get focused for the game. Still, it's a shame that they don't get a chance to see a little of the Twin Cities. There may not be enough time to really explore the area, but there is ample opportunity to get a condensed, processed version of it. There is a place here where everything that exists in nature and culture is artificially duplicated and conveniently located.

It may seem odd to come to a region for the first time and get a taste of it by visiting a mall. But this is not just any mall. It's the Mall of America. If you were to go through life and only step inside one mall, this would be it.

I realize upon entering the mall that I need headgear. So I buy a black cap that says, "JESSE, Mess with Me, Mess with My Governor, Minnesota's Governing Body." Feeling the power of "The Body," I'm ready to wrestle the mall, but where to go from here, it's hard to say. If I start in the middle, I'm immersed in Knott's Camp Snoopy, a ride-whirling, kid-screaming, indoor amusement park. The perimeter is where it's at. It's where you mall 'til you fall. Imagine a shop, and it's here. It's also got things you might not imagine, like an aquarium, a comedy club, a Northwest Airlines ticket counter, and a branch campus of National American University.

While there's much more than this, I'm hungry. So I hit the food court. At the Minnesota Picnic, there's "walleye pike on a stick," but I'm afraid it may taste more like "ditch carp on a stick." So I check out a place across the way. It's the "Cajun Cafe Grill," owned and run by a family of Chinese Americans. I can't imagine a Chinese restaurant run by Cajuns, but I shouldn't stereotype. I should sample. The owners smile big and offer a taste of Bourbon Chicken, their staple. I've never even heard of south Louisiana Bourbon Chicken, but if I had, I wouldn't have imagined it as chicken coated in soy sauce and other Chinese, er, Cajun spices. This Asian-Acadian food is tasty, but it's not native, so I head back to Minnesota Picnic and sink my teeth into that walleye pike on a stick. Conclusion: it could use a little Chino-Cajun influence.

Ever since I hit Minnesota, I've been troubled by their stereotype of the Cajun people. The Cajun Cafe Grill is only the latest example. The first was an establishment I saw in a newspaper ad called, "The Cajun Club," featuring "totally nude dancers." Some Minnesota guy must think that all Cajun ladies are hot, spicy strippers. This club certainly fits with the prurient feelings I'm starting to get about an area I thought was all about wholesome Scandinavian blondes, ice fishing, and the Lutheran ethic. My first sense of debauchery at large was an article that I saw in this morning's *Star Tribune*. The headline read, "In Coon Rapids, the Sex Party is Over." After reading the story about police busting up an open sex party, I've concluded that someone should open up a Bourbon Street burlesque club called, "The Minnesota Melon Patch," and serve shish kabobs of pike and Chinese chicken.

The more I think about it the better off the Saints are, staying in their hotel and avoiding any lewd cultural confusion. It's best they concentrate on the game and not be tempted by places like The Cajun Club. It's time for them to put to use all their hard work in Cajun Country and defend the honor of their fans, many of whom have been wrongfully stereotyped.

~

Saturday, August 5, 2000, 5:30 p.m.

Purple, purple, everywhere is purple. The Metrodome should be the Purpledome. Purple passion, purple pride, purple power. It's the solid purple seats. They're so purple they create one sweeping, shimmering purplescape. It's so purple you can feel it in your stomach, see it when you close your eyes. It's a purple haze, and it has caught Coop by the collar. He's standing on the turf, stretching, trying to contain his crunk. "Crunked," he says. "That's my word. That's a Texas word. Get crunked. Get hyped. Get motivated. Get your piss hot."

Coop is all hot to sneak a peek at the most famous current Purple People Eater. He's anxious to get a glimpse of the wrecking ball of a d-lineman who started his career as an undrafted rook and will probably end his affiliation with the league in the Hall of Fame. Wild Man John Randle is Coop's fellow Texan and his football idol. He's a man that they say Coop looks like, plays like. "That's my man," says Coop. "I can't wait to meet him. See what he look like. See if I can mimic him some kind of way. See if I can learn something from him."

As Coop looks for Randle, he takes in the dome. It seems small, like a living room. It's a campy covered saucer compared to the galaxy of the Louisiana Superdome. It's hard to believe that Randy Moss has the space to do his acrobatics in here. Then, as the seats start to fill, and some of the purple actually disappears, the place transforms. It turns into the crowded, raucous hull of an Old Norse ship. The Viking horn blows, and the purple folk roar. Ragnar rides out on his motorcycle, and the decibel meter goes through the roof. The packed crowd isn't treating this like a preseason game.

As the Vikings rumble through the tunnel, it's hard to look at them and not see Fran Tarkenton running around, pitching it to Chuck Foreman, slinging it to Ahmad Rashad and Sammy White.

In the first quarter, the Saints' defense is looking at something more imposing than the Vikes of old. They're looking at a 266-pound linebacker-for-a-quarterback in Daunte Culpepper and at the best receiving tandem in the league in Moss and Chris Carter. In the second quarter, Moss shows his freakish ability by catching a deep pass and pogo sticking over Darren Perry before falling on the two-yard line and setting up a score.

Because of two Vikings' scores before halftime, Pete Destefano gets in the game on two kickoff return teams. He's feeling a little better, having made a big pass-breakup in Thursday's practice, having heard these words from Venturi, "Pete, that's damn good, Pete. That's the way to play." The words felt good, the ball hitting his hand and falling away from the receiver felt better. But that was at safety, which is home. This is on kick return, and this is different. It's the hardest block in football, running half-backward, half-sideways, trying to find your designated person to hit who is charging full speed forward, smelling blood.

On the first return, Pete misses his initial man, but doesn't monkey around. He lets go of the fruit and finds someone else to block. On the second return, he awkwardly can't locate anyone. He's got all this pop, and he can't find anybody to smack.

With 5:09 to play in the second quarter, Chase Raynock lines up at right guard. From play one, his every move is tenacious. His pass blocking is rock solid, though his run blocking is only so-so.

Then, with 1:08 to play before halftime, the Saints line up at the Minnesota 46. On the next four plays, all passes, Chase holds his defenders at bay, keeping them away from quarterback Aaron Brooks as he drives the offense into field goal range. After Doug Brien kicks a 36-yarder as the half expires to bring the score to Saints 10, Vikings 14, Chase proudly trots off the field.

In the second half, Jamal Brooks gets into the game on the first defensive series. He is ready. "I don't know," he says. "I just had a calmness over me, even though it was a lot of people, and it was LOUD. It was my first time in that situation, in a big crowd, all that stuff, you know."

He's right. The noise doesn't phase him. He says he's calm, but he's hopping out there. The Jamal juice is flowing. On a crucial third-and-one, he whips his block, charges into the hole and drops the running back for no gain.

Later in the third quarter, Coop is doing some crazy things. At right end, he sees a pass and doesn't rush but *drops* into coverage. It's as if he's an oversized corner. It seems nuts, but it's the trend, lineman firing back and covering a zone. They call it "fire zone." Even his position coach doesn't like it. D-linemen should be running at the quarterback, trying to kill him, not backpedaling. On the fourth play of the drive, Coop seems to settle down when a play goes away from him, and he chases down the tailback. It's a play not every d-lineman can make.

Coop, though, appears a little confused on a couple of plays. He's had to learn to play tackle, to play end, to play special teams, to cover passes. In college, he was just a tackle, a head-busting tackle. Now, he's everything, everything on a bum ankle that he still won't admit is bum. He can't admit it because there's too much at stake. Not now, not with a window opening Thursday when the team released defensive end Troy Wilson, a four-game starter last year. Coop knows they're trying to cut all the Ditka that they don't like out of this team, down to the last cigar butt. So damn the ankle and damn all the perplexities. It's time to play.

Just before the end of the third quarter, the Vikings score again, and this is not good for the Saints, but it's great for Pete, who gets another shot at a kick return. This time, he's gonna take a shovel and dig the monkey hole wider, grab the freaking fruit, and not have to worry about letting it go or getting hit on the head with a stick. The fruit is his. So when the ball shoots up to the ceiling, he runs sideways, backpedals, squares, and drives his man aside. The block is textbook true.

This game is humming now. It's the real game, the fourth quarter. Some say preseason games are meaningless, but this place is brimming with meaning. To every man on this field, every play is D-Day. It could be either the first of many great ones for years to come or the last one they'll remember. They know that. They know they're fighting to play on Sundays, fighting not to spend the rest of their lives barbecuing on Sundays. It doesn't get any more meaningful than this.

Chase christens the quarter by lining up catercorner from someone he watched as a 13-year-old punk. Over there at end is Bryce Paup, who may be on his last legs, but he's still Bryce Paup. He's still the 1995 Defensive Player of Year of the entire NFL. Chase thought about playing ol' Paup before the game, thought about what it would be like to block a man who has rung up 73 career sacks. But now, Paup's in there, and Chase doesn't know it. When Paup rushes, Chase cuts him off, and he doesn't even realize it. Doesn't know who he's blocking. Won't know he's stopped Paup from touching the QB until he sees the film. His efforts on Paup and the others during the drive end in a touchdown. The Saints have closed the gap to two, 19-21.

On the ensuing kickoff, Jamal finds himself starting across from one of his best friends in the world, ex-Hampton teammate, Antico Dalton. He yells at Dalton, "You don't want none of this!"

Dalton yells back, "*You* don't want none of this! Haa! I'm gonna get it!"

Jamal shakes his head. "*I'm* gonna get it!"

Jamal thinks it can't get any better than this, lining up in an NFL game, playing against his best podnah and fellow Pirate. Then it does get better. Jamal tackles the kick returner, then helps the defense hold them to three and out. All of a sudden, he's getting it and getting it good.

On the next offensive series, Chase is in a zone. He's protecting. He's driving. He isn't smash-mouth on the running plays yet, just doesn't seem to have the power for it. But he's giving it his all, and he's moving the chains. With 4:21 to go, Doug Brien's out there again, and he drills it again. Chase looks up from his block, raises his arms, pumps his fist. Saints 22-21. He accepts a congrats from starting guard Tom Ackerman, from Haslett. He hits the bench and chats up The Truth, fills up Willie Roaf's ear. Roaf smiles. It's a big moment for the rook.

During the ensuing kickoff, Pete sprints down the field and feels the pleasure of solid contact. He tackles the returner, ends the threat. But on defense, he's not getting any action. He's covering well. Nothing, though, is flying his way, no balls, no ballcarriers. Balls are flying, however, at the defensive unit in general, and the Saints allow the Vikings to march close and kick another field goal. Vikings 24-22.

With 1:29 left in the whole shooting match, an old six-shooter enters the game at quarterback. Billy Joe Tolliver has seen a lot of snaps in 10 years with 5 different NFL teams, but he hasn't seen one down of action in the preseason. He didn't play at all in the scrimmage. The coaches keep saying they already know what he can do. They will certainly know now. They'll get a good dose of ol' B.J., ol' Joe, ol' Fire Head. So the ol' Red Raider hitches up for what could be his last ride, and he rallies a bunch of rookies and ragtags and turns them into a driving machine. He steers the chuck wagon 43 yards in 4 plays to the Vikings' 31. When ol' Red stops, there are only three ticks left in the rodeo.

As Doug Brien jogs out to attempt the game winner, yet another redhead is watching, and his emotions are all jumbled up. Shayne Graham has been playing this game for eight years, and in each of those years, this kick has always been his. Before this game, he thought this one would be his. The fourth quarter belonged to him. That's what they'd told him.

/ TWELVE /

TRAINER!

Now, the coaches have changed their mind. It's not Shayne's kick anymore. They told him so two minutes before Brien's last kick, told him it was Doug's show from this point forward. So as Brien runs out there for the big one, Shayne's feelings are "hard to explain. I mean, I was hopeful for him to make it," he would say later, "but I don't want to say jealous. That's not the word. Definitely, not jealous, but it was like I really wish I was the one getting the opportunity to do that. He's been here for years. He earned it. But I was really hungry for it."

He's hungry because history says he won't miss it. In four years of high school and in four years of college, he never failed to deliver. If the snap went back with the game on the line, Graham was always golden. The only potential game winner he missed had no consequence. His Virginia Tech Hokies won the game in overtime anyway. Every other time, the ball sailed true. Every other time, Graham put all the hulks on his back and carried them to victory.

Then there was that one time, a moment when all of Hokiedom held their breath, a kick he had to make, a pendulum that had to swing Tech's way to elevate the university to a place it had never been in its 127-year existence. It may be unfair that football can give so much prestige to a proud academic institution. But it's true. Legendary coach Bear Bryant was dead-on when he said it's a little hard to rally around a math program. Math? Well, Tech had all the Calc. and Diff. Eq. anyone could ever need. But it didn't have an undefeated season. It never had the chance to play in the national title game. It didn't have the jolt it needed to move out of the shadow of that school that Thomas Jefferson designed in Charlottesville.

Tech might've had the best quarterback in the land in Michael Vick, that freshman wunderkind. But on the chilly night in Morgantown, Super Vick could only take the Hokies so far. He could only drive them down to the West Virginia 27, with just enough time in the game left for one play to erase a 19-20 deficit. To win this one, Vick needed Shayne Graham. So did his coach, Frank Beamer, so did every athlete that had ever worn the Hokie maroon and orange, from Bruce Smith to Ace Custis, so did those math professors, so did every gal with VT painted on her cheek and so did every die-hard Hokie from Wytheville to Williamsburg.

So as their nerves shot up and down, Shayne calmly eyed the bottom third of the ball. It didn't matter that this was enemy territory, and that the Mountaineer fans were wearing their throats out screaming. Shayne was in a comfortable place. And when he struck the leather, and it split the uprights just as the final gun sounded, Morgantown went quiet, and Hokiedom went berserk. The force of the kick echoed into every coal mine, across every tobacco field, up every hill and down every holler, blasting through the Appalachians all the way to Blacksburg. The season's last three games were a foregone conclusion. The redhead had given them deliverance. Virginia Polytechnic Institute and State University had arrived.

But, now, here in this enclosed den of Minnesota madness, Shayne can't smell the coal dust or the pine trees. There isn't a blue ridge anywhere in sight. There's just Doug Brien standing on the carpet, kicking his field goal.

And kick it straight he does! Chase Raynock looks up from his block and jumps. He becomes a part of a black and gold celebration that might as well be a playoff win. As he turns toward the stands, where his family and high school coach are sitting, he's a long way from that Jets game where he moped his way through the Meadowlands. He's asked, "What a turn of events, huh?"

"Fuck yeah," he exclaims. "I came out, and I played a hell of a game. And I feel so good about tonight. It's a great, great thing. We won the game. I mean this offense took it on its shoulders and won the game. That's all I gotta talk about right there. I am so happy right now."

He sees his mother waving her arms. He's giving her that baby boy, look-at-the-frog-I-just-caught smile. "I'm just happy," he says, gushing. "I'm just so happy right now."

He reaches up to the rail and hoists his little brother, Jake, who is past the point of worship. "He was awesome," says Jake. "I was cheering for him the whole time. He's a big boy for a rookie." Jake sizes me up and asks, "Can you get me a game ball?"

They're all fawning over Chase—Jake, Mom, Dad, his high school coach. They've driven more than 800 miles from Billings, Montana, traversing the entire windy state of North Dakota, to see their boy play with the pros. "I'm just so happy." He can't say it enough.

Across the field, Jamal and his friend Antico Dalton have mobbed each other. They're laughing, jiving, living it up. Afterward, Jamal and his five-tackle performance come smiling my way. He sees me, "Gimme some love!" He gives me a hug and tells me, "You been there since the beginning."

I ask him about his big stop on a third and short. His response is: "God! You know, God. Actually, this week I've been trying to concentrate on my spiritual more than anything and seek the kingdom of God first. And all the rest'll fall into place, and He just proved to me today that's exactly how it's going to go. Last week, I wasn't saying I was going against and sinning, but I wasn't really focusing on Him. (Now I'm) trying to get back and read my Bible and everything."

Everything is joy in the locker room—almost everything. Desmond Gibson didn't play a down, but when he's asked about it, he's neither high nor low. He's simply the calm son of preachers. "There ain't much to say," he says. "I mean, you know, I guess that's the system. Maybe they want to take a look at some other guys that didn't get a lot of time last week. So I'll just sit back and wait for my chance again."

Desmond says he's surprised he's gone from playing more than any undrafted rookie in the Jets game to not playing at all, but will only say, "This week it was my turn to watch."

Desmond's fellow tackle, the bewildered Robert Brannon, watched for most of the game, but was glad to get in and even gladder to win as an ex-Iowa State Cyclone used to losing. "Ain't won in so long. It felt good," he says.

Across the lockers, Pete is happy the defense played well, but disappointed that the unit's strong fourth quarter performance meant less reps for him. "It sucks. I didn't get my rhythm." Also, Pete's lone stop at safety had a consequence. The hit opened the wound on his nose for the third time, and he will need more stitches. He is, in general, having a difficult time stitching it all together. "I think I'm overtrained right now. I'm not sleeping worth shit."

Sleep is something that Coop will have a difficult time obtaining on the plane ride home. His eyes are cast downward. He says he watched John Randle's every snap but didn't try to meet his idol after the game. "I was too upset," he says. "I wanted to have the best game of my life, you know, around him, and I didn't. That way I can say I played my best and go and meet him, tell him I want to be like him. And I didn't get to do that."

Looking at Coop, one wouldn't know he played decently and made two tackles. Looking across at Chase, one would see immediately that he's all tickled purple. He's got a dip of Copenhagen in his lower lip, and he's still in his uniform, even though everyone else has already showered. He'd sleep in it if they let him.

~

Sunday, August 6, 2000, 3:00 p.m.

The Saints probably don't realize how aquatically connected they are to where they've just been. Had they only walked a few blocks from the Metrodome to the Mississippi River, they'd be on the path to the foot of training camp. They could've hitched a ride on a Huck Finn-type raft in the narrow upper Mississippi, let it take them downstream through 10 states all the way to just below Baton Rouge. Then with a hard right at Donaldsonville, portaging over the levee and the pumps, they'd be in Bayou Lafourche, on which their vacation destination sits. They wouldn't be going all the way to Fourchon, where the bayou meets the Gulf and the specks and reds run all over the surf. That's too far down. The place of respite for their raft will be Camp Haslett, a few hundred yards from the bayou's slow, murky waters.

At this dead hour, Shayne Graham isn't exactly taking a leisurely rafting trip. He's spending his day off jogging. Something has driven him to put on his running shoes and hit the quiet, scalded streets of Thibodaux. It's not that he doesn't think he's bled enough oil already the last three weeks. "I don't know what possessed me," he says. It is the kind of stuff that possesses a person when something has been taken from him for the first time in his life. He is thinking about the kick that was not.

He swears he never wished that Doug Brien would've missed it. "If he misses, he misses. There's no reason for me to want that. That's just bad sportsmanship for that, and it also would screw my head up if I wanted my opportunity to come off somebody else's misfortune. That's just not the way it works, and it's not a very professional way to think about it."

He would be much better off, though, had Brien missed. He would be thinking that he still has a real chance to make this team and not about his unacceptable performances kicking off. "I know right now everybody's questioning my leg strength, and I know that's not the problem. I'm planting too close to the ball, and it's causing my leg to not to have room to work. It's basically a dead leg swinging through it, and I'm running at the ball, and that running does no good when my body is not allowed to get through it."

While Shayne is beating up his body, everyone else is doing their best to relax. Coop has used his days off to hang out with his new friends and fellow Omega Psi Phi fraternity brothers at Nicholls. Jamal Brooks is taking in a gospel play called, "Behind Closed Doors," at the Orpheum Theater in New Orleans. Last Sunday, Pete Destefano, Chase Raynock, and Robert Brannon were invited to a crab boil by some local girls that Chase befriended.

"Crab's too damn hard to eat," says Chase. "I'll tell you what, it ain't worth all the effort to get in them to eat them stupid things."

The most popular thing to do is to sleep as much as possible. The players are building up weeks of missed winks, and with the team not making it back to the dorm until 3-4 a.m. for these away games, nothing is as valuable as a little extra shut-eye.

～

Monday, August 7, 2000, 3:45 p.m.

Dark clouds are inching over the cane field, blackening the entire sky. Lightning flashes in the south, then in the southeast. It streaks on the horizon one more time, and the horn blows. The players take the signal from Haslett to jog off the field. They think practice is over. They go back to the air-conditioning of the locker room, cool down, then freeze their heavily perspired, rain-wet bodies. Just as their muscles get into the sore, postpractice mode, just as some noses start running, they're summoned out to Guidry Stadium. As they come out to the field, they aren't exactly skipping. "Makes it like two practices," says Coop.

~

Chase Raynock's dedication at practice today hasn't gone unnoticed. One person, rain or shine, has watched him closer than any coach or fellow player. Chase hasn't made a move that slipped under her smothering radar. You could call her a secret admirer, but it's hardly a secret when she has his picture laminated into the countertop of her workplace. You can't buy an electronics part at the Thibodaux Wal-Mart Supercenter without noticing three oversized prints of Chase at practice, his helmet off, of course.

When Cheri Boudreaux's mother asked her to go to the first training camp practice, she declined at first. Cheri didn't care for football. Nevertheless, she gave in and went anyway. Then, when the players started stretching, she saw something she didn't expect to see. "Oooo! Look at him," she told her mother, pointing at number 74. It was a crush at first blush.

From that point on, Cheri attended every practice she could. The young lady, who once hated sports, grew to love them. One day, Cheri and her friends were at a Wendy's just off campus when they spotted some Saints' football players. Cheri looked into the gathering of gargantuan men and felt a cold streak go through her body. She jumped and screamed, careful that Chase not see her. Her friend arranged a photo op. A 20 x 30" picture of Cheri and Chase now hangs in her living room.

"Aww, he's too cute," she says while ringing up some batteries at Wal-Mart. "And he's nice. I'd like to meet him."

"But you met him at Wendy's."

"Yeah, but I'd like to *really* meet him." She winks.

When Chase hears of his admirer's wishes, he gets an uncomfortable look on his face. It ain't easy being Elvis.

~

Tuesday, August 8, 2000, 5:00 p.m.

In a 9-on-7 drill, Jamal Brooks lowers into his stance. "I'm starting to see stuff way before it even happens," he says. He sees something here, reading the play as the center snaps the ball, then positioning himself perfectly. As the force of the offense comes his way, he shucks the fullback's block, plugs the hole, and lays a nice, cold pop on the running back.

Zook hollers, "That's a hit! Nice hit, baby!"

The horn blows. The drills break up, and the players start to salivate. The real hitting is about to begin. Every frustration, every inhibition is about to be released. All the rules about not tackling will soon be tossed. What is coming is the only full-fledged, anything-goes war that exists in practice, and it doesn't take place that often. It's goal line. It's jailbreak. It's empty the zoo, animals on the loose. It's all out, apeshit bedlam. It's ball-busting, ass-blowing football.

~

As the offense and defense dig in on the goal line, Zook is vibrating. "Get you some of this now. Get you some of this now!"

Clancy's head is bobbing, shouting, "Kick them motherfuckers' ass now!"

The offensive coaches are quietly intense, like silent pit bulls.

On the first snap, the heavy equipment thrusts and collides. From the sound of it, monster trucks might as well be crashing into each other. The defense smashes back the o-line and stops Ricky Williams before he can crest the line of scrimmage. On the second play, the offense surges, banging back the defense. Ricky is quickly over the top and into pay dirt. He spikes the ball.

For the third go-around, the personnel changes. Number one head-smasher Wilmont Perry is back there at running back. He's drooling. He knows he can do something here that Ricky, with all his talent and trophies, could never do. "Hut!" The d-line blows back the o-line, and it seems as if Perry is doomed. Nose tackle Robert Newkirk pops him first. But Perry bucks him like a mountain bighorn. He runs over Newkirk and into strong safety Gerald Vaughn, who wops him. Perry head butts Vaughn and bounces off. Next, free safety Eric Johnson squares and lays into him. Perry lowers his shoulder and keeps his feet. He's in the end zone standing up.

Before the cheer comes, there's a split second of silence. Everyone is a little awestruck. Not many backs in the NFL can make this run. It's the kind of run that happens mostly in cartoons.

Watching in admiration is Pete Destefano. Pete has had his nose busted open twice by Perry. Although Vaughn and Johnson are his competitors, he doesn't think it's their fault that Perry scored. "That was just all Wilmont," says Pete. Pete, though, has to wonder what would have happened if he'd been where they were. He has to believe that he would've bucked, wrapped up and drug down the bighorn. Yes, Perry's hits twice drew his blood, but both times, Perry came crashing to the ground.

Despite not being allowed to unleash himself on goal line, Pete is feeling better about things. He says Venturi has been paying attention to him in meetings. He's getting a few more reps now that they've moved Shannon Garrett back to cornerback. The problem is he needs as many as possible to make this team as the tenth defensive back. Four older head safeties and four older head corners are already locks to make the team. Rookie corner Michael Hawthorne will almost certainly be the ninth d-back because, one, he's a draft pick. And, two, his play has steadily improved.

So for the tenth d-back's spot, Pete'll have to battle the Canadians, who aren't really Canadians but Mississippians who are veterans of the Canadian Football League. Garrett, an ex-Mississippi College star who is from just down the way in Bay St. Louis, has played north of the border for five seasons. He has been impressive here as a ball-hawking corner. Vaughn, of Abbeville, Mississippi and Ole Miss, has competed in Grey Cup country the last seven years. He's had an outstanding camp and made a name for himself with a punt block in the Minnesota game. Garrett and Vaughn, though, share the same liability—age. At 28 and 30, respectively, they're almost old men by NFL standards.

While Johnson is also 28, the Maben, Mississippi native only has three years of CFL wear and tear on his body. Johnson hasn't been as effective as Vaughn and Garrett, but at 6-4, 218, he's a tall presence, who actually played linebacker and rush end in Canada.

Pete sees Johnson as his main competitor, mostly because they both play free safety. Although the competition is bestial, Pete likes Johnson. Just last night, Johnson gave him a ride to a bank to deposit some money. They then grabbed a burger together. Pete discovered that Johnson has an interesting story. After playing initially at Holmes Junior College in Mississippi, Johnson accepted a scholarship to Idaho State. In the potato state, the African-American southerner not only found a place to play football, he found a wife, a white wife.

During the off-season, Johnson and his wife live with her family on a ranch in Gooding, Idaho. The family business is rodeo production, which for Johnson means doing chores that include feeding the cattle and horses and driving tractors. He's also had to get outside jobs because the most he's made in the CFL is about $30,000 in American dollars. He's worked at a cheese plant and, of course, at a potato plant.

Johnson, Garrett, and Vaughn have seen a lot of Canada, and if at all possible, they don't want to return. They're ready to play NFL football and make NFL dollars. "This is The Show," says Johnson. "This is where everybody want to be, everybody in the CFL, World League, no matter what, Arena football. Everybody wants to be down here."

Pete wants to be here, too, but to stay here, he must outwant and outplay three others who are motivated by the desire not to go back to the land of frostbite, hypothermia, and high taxes. Pete has youth. They have experience. All four have NFL talent, but only one, maybe none, will stay.

~

Wednesday, August 9, 2000, 9:35 a.m.

If it hadn't already, reality has struck. It's the realization that happens during the middle of the fourth week of a tedium that at times approaches lunacy. It's when you realize that despite all the tents, plastic footballs, and pink bears, it's still steaming outside. Despite all the Gatorade, grandstands, and applause, practice is still practice.

Even with all the rope tricks, kiddie obstacle courses, and corporate promotions, camp becomes a grind for everyone involved, even the media. Even as the scribes find new, creative angles for their stories, eventually it's overkill. Even the bands, the Saintsations, and all the beer at Rox's and Bubba's combined can't turn this into something novel at this point. It's just training camp. And unless you're a coach, it's just too long.

If any player should have a true idea of how long camp should be, it's The Truth himself, All-Decade Willie Roaf. "It's a little long this year," says Roaf. "We haven't had one this long in a couple of years. You know, when you're dealing with this heat, you start getting a little tired after awhile, but it's been a productive camp. We've been pretty healthy for the most part. I just think it has been a little long. I think a good three weeks is enough."

Center Jerry Fontenot is going through his twelfth training camp. "I know historically the reasons for training camp, and that was (when) guys didn't do anything in the off-season," says Fontenot. "They came into (camp) to get in shape and get ready for the season when they had other jobs. Now, this is our job. We're here from March 27 until whenever, January whenever." Fontenot says that the spring conditioning, mini-camps, and coaching sessions have, for the most part, prepared their bodies and minds for the season. Consequently, a lengthy camp is unnecessary. "I think 21 days would be plenty," he says.

"I think you can ask any ballplayer, and they'd say training camp is too long," says five-year veteran defensive tackle, La'Roi Glover. "It's a grind, but I think it's a process of just weeding guys out and getting them prepared for the long season."

Glover believes that two weeks of camp would be sufficient. "I think guys are in such good shape now. They train year-round. They don't need the long camp. It's not like the old days where guys waited for a week or two before the season started to get themselves in shape."

This morning's practice is losing its shape, and the coaches sense it. While the players dawdle from drill to drill, Zook is an out of control power tool, sawing and drilling and sanding up the grass. Next to his hyperactivity, the players look like mimes and mannequins. Their lax motion must be partially due to the heat, which is especially taxing this morning and appears to be causing some to stumble off to the sidelines with cramping and dizziness.

Meanwhile, Zook's mouth keeps fluttering, and from time to time, he fires a few sentences intended to work like smelling salts. He hollers:

"See, you're even drinking slow. Move fast."

"Come on. This is hard shit. There's no time to be tired."

"Keep competing. Keep competing, baby. That's why they keep score in this game."

One person who is visibly competing is Randy Mueller. He's not doing it with his legs and forearms, though. His weapon is a cell phone. He's been on it, off and on, all through practice. In less than two weeks, he will have to trim 12 players from the roster in what will be the first big cut. But given his history, a trade or a cut could come at any time. His unpredictability is heightened by the fact that he hasn't been at practice the last couple of days.

Now, he's there, and he's standing next to the Turk. They're talking about something. The Turk is nodding. Anything could happen at any time.

In the short run, practice ends two hours after it begins. This has been camp's shortest practice and it should be, considering that in Haslett's words, there were "a whole bunch of" his players who suffered dehydration this morning. He admits, "It was brutal out there."

~

Eight hours later, under the lights and cooler temperatures at Guidry Stadium, the titans are clashing. The lead is dramatic, but in truth, the action isn't, not on the surface anyway. The evening session doesn't appear to be any spryer than the morning practice. The crowd even seems half asleep. Nevertheless, the battle among the undrafted rookies on the defensive line is still raging. Clancy still sees the athletic, fuel-injected Coop as the favorite, but the gap has narrowed. "I tell you who's coming along is really Brannon," says Clancy. "He's a force in the middle when he do things right, and if he uses his hands and his feet (better), who knows?"

Robert Brannon isn't much of a force tonight. He's sitting out practice with a sore back but expects to return tomorrow.

Once again, Coop is trying to be too forceful. Clancy says that Coop has to start cutting down on his mental mistakes, but in tonight's one-on-one drills, he makes another one. He jumps offside two times in a row. After the second penalty, he flails his arms and belts, "Aaaa! Fuck!"

As for Desmond Gibson, he is starting to look more comfortable. He's using his hands more, but he's still not shedding his blocks fast enough. He doesn't quite have the NFL rhythm. And if anybody understands rhythm, it's Desmond. He's always carried the beat as a drummer boy. He started playing at age eight in church, and as he grew older, he started "laying tracks," "putting a little beat together here and there." His favorite music is jazz, but he also plays gospel, R&B, anything. It's easy for him to feel the beat of a song, to copy it, to create his own.

The NFL, however, isn't quite like his drum set yet. Since the beginning of camp, he's talked about wanting to get better every day, yet in talking to him, you don't feel that he has a sense of urgency. It may be that he's not revealing it due to his even nature. But surely he knows that improvement alone won't cut it here. If he is to have any chance of making the roster, he needs an NFL caliber performance in this Saturday night's game.

As for last Saturday's game, Desmond acted as if he was unaffected by not playing. But it had to affect him. He is, after all, Desmond Gibson, a name that once meant everything in western Pennsylvania. Western Pennsylvania is to football what Indiana is to basketball, what the Dominican Republic is to baseball, what Quebec is to hockey. Football is as vital to the region's spirit as steel is to its economy, and it seems to produce as many quality football players as it does tons of top-grade steel.

In 1995, Desmond was arguably the best of the best in Western P-A. As a jackhammering offensive lineman and a detonating defensive lineman, he put his Penn Hills High team on his shoulders and carried them to a 15-0 season and a state championship. His chip was true blue, and his mailbox was chocked-full of recruiting letters. He made national recruiting lists at o-line and d-line. He could've gone anywhere he wanted, but chose to stay home at Pitt. He turned down Joe Pa and Penn State and four years of guaranteed winning for one main reason—playing time. At Pitt, he knew he would play right away. And that's exactly what happened. In four years as a Panther, he never failed to play in a game. So what happened to him last Saturday night in the Metrodome has never happened to him.

As Desmond lines up tonight here in Guidry Stadium in one-on-ones and jumps offside, it's got to be hard to stay the modest son of preachers. It's got to be frustrating not to have played when it's so important to you that the probability of playing immediately was the deciding factor in where you went to college. It's got to eat at the man, scripture or no scripture, peaceful upbringing or no peaceful upbringing, jazz CDs or no jazz CDs. Even smooth Dizzy G. can't completely drown out what happened in Minneapolis, that feeling of watching your team win and knowing you didn't have a hand in it, that lingering question about whether a team has any plans to keep a guy who doesn't play a down.

Even with these internal battles raging in Desmond and many others, externally, practice is dead. It's actually moving at a decent clip, but nothing unusual is happening—nothing, that is, until The Word. It is the one utterance that brings everything to a halt. Otherwise, it is a rare moment for even Haslett to stop the action. The practice schedule is all pretimed, with ol' Silky blowing the air horn at set increments. The horn makes its noise, and they move, but they don't stop—ever. Ever, until the word that is. And dead smack in the middle of a quiet short yardage drill, here it comes:

TRAINER!!!

Everything halts. There's a scrum around a body. The trainers charge in, and the scrum dissipates. Yes, it's all stopped, but now it's moving again. In less than 20 seconds, the cease-fire ends. The drill moves down the field, away from the fallen. Up in the stands, you finally see a number. You see a "7," then a "4," and your stomach tightens. Not Chase, not one of ours. One minute, ol' Big Sky is in NFL full-pad-practice-one, and he's mashed into cream potatoes by Jared Tomich. The next, he's learning, getting better, only to have his excitement of wearing the uniform ruined by hardly playing against the Jets. Then, he's redeemed, pushing the Purple People Eaters away from his quarterback, helping to pull his team to victory. *Now this.*

Each trainer takes an arm. They hoist him, holding up his left leg. The crowd claps for him. A ball boy wheels in a little John Deere pulling a wagon, and they lay Chase in it. Whatever's wrong with that left leg is making him wince. Dr. Maki's back there with him, talking as much encouragement as he is orthopedics.

Chase is laying there, sucking in this strange, thick air, almost two thousand miles from home and a thousand-plus from his Metrodome glory. He doesn't know what's causing the pain. All he can do is wait for the film. All he can do is wait to see what fate the MRI will reveal.

/ THIRTEEN /

ME, TEAM

Thursday, August 10, 2000, 3:15 p.m.

Up above, a cauldron of thunderheads is brewing and bubbling. The sky is ripe with raw electricity. Black masses are forming, thickening and moving toward the practice fields from every direction. Lightning strikes in the east, then in the west. It is dancing now, from one end of the horizon to the other. The air horn sounds. The troops run for cover.

While the players are in danger, they are not as exposed as the videographers who film their every move. At each practice, three men stand on the decks of cherry pickers jacked 40 feet high. One of them is Bob Lee, the Saints' assistant video director. "I'm never scared of lighting, which I guess is stupid," says Lee. "I'm always surprised when they tell me to go down."

At this instant, as he jacks down his cherry picker, he thinks the storms are too far away. "We've shot in worse conditions than that. I remember with Coach Ditka we were out there in a tropical storm shooting, practically, and he didn't let us come down until the team came off the field. And we were just totally drenched, and the storm had already hit."

Approaching storms aren't all bad for Lee. It adds a little variety to what can be a mundane routine. At every practice session, he shoots the end zone camera, and his boss, Joe Motta, shoots the sideline. They have to bring the equipment out to the field an hour before practice to get the cameras adjusted to the heat and the humidity. Once practice starts, he must keep the daydreaming to a minimum.

"When you're shooting, you have to know what the coaches are looking for and keep the proper frame and the right people in the picture. As a casual spectator, your focus, you know, your interest can come and go."

There are many days when Lee would rather be filming Saintsations tryouts. "You watch much more of practice than you really like to." Nevertheless, if you have to watch practice, it's arguably the best seat available. "People think that we're a lot hotter up in the air on those metal lifts, but it's actually pretty nice 'cause you can catch the breeze up there."

There's nothing breezy about Lee's training camp schedule. During a two-a-day, Lee's day starts at 6:30 a.m. and ends at midnight. A one-a-day goes from about 9 a.m. 'til 7 p.m. When Lee and Motta and the video team aren't shooting, they're editing. When they're not editing, they're attending the same meetings the players attend just in case something goes wrong with the equipment or if a coach needs a certain tape.

During practice, after each drill is over, Lee and the other videographers place their Beta videos of the drill into a net and drop them down to runners who take the videos to the editors for immediate editing and dubbing. The editors must "intercut" all of the team drills, splicing together an end zone view and a sideline angle of each play. The editors must work quickly. "As soon as the coaches come back after practice, they want to start looking at the tapes." By the end of the day, they'll go through about 100 tapes.

While all the editing at camp is done on tape-to-tape decks, back at the Saints' facility, the editing is performed on a $250,000 Avid SportsPro. Also, each assistant coach has a $25,000 Avid Coach's Station at his disposal so he can discard the unnecessary clips and conduct his meetings as efficiently as possible.

After preseason games, the video team outworks every man in the organization. When the team returns from a game, and everyone goes to sleep, the video guys stay up all night, intercutting the game and making dubs. They have to immediately ship tapes to the Saints' next three opponents, to the NFL "Dub Center," and to all the Saints' coaches and front office personnel.

At the moment, the next preseason game isn't on Bob Lee's mind as he hustles off the field with his camera. He's more interested in shielding his expensive hardware. Ten minutes after Lee and the rest of the Saints' staffers are safe and dry, the sky empties, sending walls of water down in a deluge.

In the Barker Hall locker facility, the players listen to the rain pound the roof and worry that they'll either have to return to the field when it stops raining or get bused to the Houma-Terrebonne Civic Center to conclude practice on the turf. When Haslett calls them together, they fear the worst. He tells them, "Two buses will be here in about 15 minutes."

There is a collective, "Uhhh," from the players. They think they're going to Houma. Haslett then tells them the buses are going to take them across campus to Ellender Dormitory. For the first time all camp, he cancels practice and evening meetings and tells them they're free until midnight. They whoop and hoot. The taste of freedom, even temporary freedom, is sweet.

One player who feels anything but free is Chase Raynock. He's currently confined to crutches and a left knee brace. Lightning has already struck him, and the results are mixed. He has subluxed his patella, meaning his kneecap popped out of its groove and then popped back into it. His knee is so swollen he can't bend it or extend it. Fortunately, though, the MRI is negative. The sprain is severe, but it's only a sprain.

"Only" is a relative term. In this case, he's definitely out for Saturday night's game against the Colts at Purdue University in West Lafayette, Indiana. He's probably out for a good 10 days, but he's hoping he'll be back for the last preseason game against Miami, which is 15 days away.

The injury occurred when he was blocking down on the tackle and a defender came from behind and rolled up on his knee. His leg gave out on him, and he crashed to the ground. His pain is still pretty intense. He's trying not to think about the painful uncertainty the injury has created.

～

Saturday, August 12, 2000, 12:00 p.m.

Once again, the players are suffocating. They're holed up in a corporate hotel, surrounded by the urban sprawl of Indianapolis. They could be staying in a place of natural strength, an hour up the road from the city. It's a place nestled in rolling countryside quilted with corn and beans, accented by silver silos and rustic barns and intoned with the sounds of basketball bouncing in the dirt. For every John Wooden, Rick Mount, and Big Dog Robinson that hooped it up at Purdue, there's a Len Dawson, a Leroy Keyes, and a Mike Alstott. And for every Rod Woodson and Drew Brees, there's a Neil Armstrong and a Gus Grissom.

Purdue is the school of astronauts and engineers, agronomists and athletes. It's where the Saints should've been today. They should've stayed at the hallowed Club Hotel in Memorial Union so they could now walk among the tall oaks and maples and the red brick buildings, listen to the bells chime and the cicadas drone. They could have found ways to draw inspiration from a university not associated with their training camp, to rekindle what made them so loose and good in their college days, to take an old Saturday afternoon performance and replicate it tonight.

Instead, they're in their sterile hotel rooms, or they're taking a brief jaunt through the manufactured air of the mall connected to their hotel. They could be out here in this cool, blue day in a place hued as black and gold as their game uniforms. They could take in a meal at the lunch counter at Ehresman's Triple "XXX" and sit across from a couple that looks Amish, but is actually German Baptist. They could end their feast with a banana split from Frozen Custard, a neon, timeless place across the Wabash River in Lafayette.

But this isn't about a town that is a 37,762-student school. It's the corporate NFL at work. It's Purdue University being crazy enough to guarantee the Colts and the Saints $500,000 apiece and then not sell nearly enough tickets to break even. One can't blame an Indianan if they don't want to shell out $20 or $35 or $55 to watch an exhibition, not when the real thing is going on across the river at the Colt World Series or on the river itself at the USCA National Canoe and Kayak Marathon Championships. For $3, area sports fans can catch a double-header at Loeb Stadium featuring Pembroke Pines, FL vs. Rapid City,

SD and Santa Clara, CA vs. the Lafayette All-Stars. For free, they can sit on the riverbank, drink beer, and watch all the world-class canoeing and kayaking they can bear.

On the western side of the river, the high-paying customers are standing in a less than one-third-full Ross-Ade Stadium, waiting for the Purdue football team to sing the national anthem. Compared to the Saints and Colts, the Boilermakers appear to be the size of high schoolers. They prove their manhood by giving a deep, testosterone-filled version of the "Star Spangled Banner."

Next, the Indianapolis cheerleaders prance out to midfield and spell C-O-L-T-S with their fine figures and white pom-poms. Watching with amusement are our eight heroes. Little do they know that for almost all of them, this is as good as it will get tonight.

In the first half, the Colts' former undrafted rookie receiving tandem almost single-handedly sinks the Saints as Indianapolis takes the lead 14-0. Colts wide receiver Terrence Wilkins and tight end Marcus Pollard catch seven of Peyton Manning's nine first-half passes and account for 63% of Indianapolis' total offensive yardage.

For the Saints' undrafted rookies, the first half and most of the second are excruciating. They're not being called out to the field, and there certainly isn't anything pleasant for them to watch. For some of them, they're just up the road from a place associated with their draft demise. Earlier this year, they were in the Hoosier state at the RCA Dome in Indianapolis for the NFL scouting combine's annual workout. Team representatives attend the workout and watch more than 300 invited players go through a series of tests, none of which involve putting on the pads and playing football.

D. J. Cooper, Robert Brannon, and Shayne Graham were all there. Robert called the experience a "blur." Coop and Shayne don't have fond memories of it, and both believe their subpar workouts there are what put the dagger in their draft chances.

"(Cooper's) combine workouts were horrible," said Mike Detillier. "He didn't run well. His agility 'deal' drills were not very good, and it devastated him. It devastated any chances of him getting drafted."

Right now, Coop and the rest of the undrafted rookies only want the chance to play football, and they're not getting it. The highlight of the second half is Bill LaFleur's punting. While one pooch attempt hits the Colts' 20-yard line, he nails his other attempt on the two-yard line. For Bill's mates, only Coop and Jamal get in the game, and they don't get in there until there are five minutes and thirty-two seconds left in the fourth quarter. Coop makes the most of his one-series opportunity by making two tackles. Shayne, Desmond, Robert, and Pete don't play at all.

The Colts win 17-0, and few of the 20,105 in attendance seem to care.

After the game, walking off the field, Shayne Graham says he was supposed to kick in the fourth quarter, had the Saints' offense given him the opportunity. "I don't know what's going on right now as far as where my holding on the team is," he says. "I'll take what I can get."

His reaction to Doug Brien's missed field goal is decidedly different than it's been in the past. "If that opens more opportunity for me and makes the door a little wider for me, then that's great. I mean, I hate to see him fail and all that, but if it helps me out, if it opens the door for me, I hope to capitalize on it. If it doesn't, so be it."

In the visitor's locker room, it's a cramped, steamy, uncomfortable scene. It's difficult to maneuver in a tight crowd of naked, angry giants. As I knife my way through, Desmond Gibson sees me and says, "I ain't got nothing to say."

"Nothing to say?" I respond.

"No."

"That says enough."

"What type of questions could you ask?"

"I just want to know what you were thinking."

"Same thing as last week. Take every quote from last week and use it for this week."

Nothing about his present temperament says he's the even son of preachers. It would even be difficult for St. Francis to maintain a sense of peace in Desmond's situation. Across the room, Pete Destefano's mood is understandably not much different than Desmond's.

"Tough game," I tell him.

"Yeah," he says. "I mean not a whole lot to say, really."

He tries to put a positive spin on it. "Coach (Venturi) told me that, unless he's lying, and I don't know, but he said that I'll be playing quite a bit in the next game so I'm excited. It's at home." He pauses. "I mean, it's the first time that I've never gotten in any football game before in my whole life. That part was hard.

"I don't know. It's hard on me. It's hard on a lot of people. That's really all I got to say."

Jamal Brooks has a little more to say. He knew going in that the starters were going to play more, and he would play less. He mentally prepared himself for it. "The only thing I can control is myself, and when I got in, I felt like I did what I had to do," he says. "I mean it's not up to me. I can't control all that other stuff. I can't control when I'm getting in. I can't control none of that. I just leave that up to God."

As Jamal got antsy waiting on the sideline for his opportunity, he watched his roommate and best friend on the team, Joe Tuipala, play a significant amount of time at linebacker. Although the two are competing for the same spot, they have helped each other get better since the first day of camp. They are the first to arrive at the film room every morning. They give each other pointers during practice and in games. When Jamal is asked whether it was awkward seeing Tuipala get the shot he would have liked to have had, he responds, "No, that's gonna be my friend forever."

At the other end of the locker room, Robert Brannon gives his thoughts about the game. "I'm disappointed in both things—I didn't play, and we lost. More in that we lost, though, man. I hate losing. I don't like that, man."

Robert is apparently thinking "team" here. He doesn't understand that this game has nothing to do with "team." It has everything to do about "me." It's not TEAM, me; it's ME, team. It has to be. That's not selfishness. It's survival. Once the season starts, and you're on that roster, and you're collecting your game check, then it's about the team. Then it's okay to sit the bench, if sitting the bench gives the Saints a better chance to win. But as for now, your pursuit is an individual sport disguised as a team game.

This game is not good for our heroes. It can't be. When it comes to earning a spot on the roster, nothing positive can come from not playing. The first big cut could happen as early as Monday morning. It must happen by a week from Tuesday. With there being no game next weekend, the undrafted rookies have little opportunity to prove themselves before the first cut. They needed this game, and they didn't get it. Maybe later they can turn this experience into a life lesson. But that's got nothing to do with the here and now. It's got nothing to do with the two weeks that could be the rest of their lives. Not a damn thing to do with it.

/ FOURTEEN /

THE LAST MOON RISES

Sunday, August 13, 2000, 4:40 a.m.

The man doesn't know it, but in a few hours, he will be tested. Something is happening at this very moment that will affect him, affect his team. He will be forced to deal with an issue he's not yet dealt with as a head coach. It will be a matter different than inept preseason performances or season-ending injuries. It is something that inevitably he would have had to face. The law of averages dictates as much. One can't coach 80 to 90 players and not have one of them stray.

Right now, one is allegedly straying. A Kenner police officer is driving in his squad car on Williams Boulevard, and he's watching a Land Rover swerve. He would later learn that the vehicle belongs to Saints' safety Darren Perry, who is less than two hours removed from landing in the team plane at the airport. The officer continues to observe Perry's vehicle weave, then strike a curb, kicking up his two front tires into the air and landing in a parking lot.

The policeman orders Perry out of the car. He smells alcohol and gives Perry a field sobriety test. Perry fails it. Perry refuses a breath-alcohol test and exercises his right to remain silent. The officer arrests Perry for driving while intoxicated and books him. Minutes after the arrest, he later learns Perry had allegedly committed another action earlier that morning that has legal consequences. Not long before Perry's DWI arrest, he allegedly rear-ended a motorist at the intersection of Clay Street and Airline Highway, then fled the scene. After the collision, Perry had reportedly gotten out of his Land Rover, walked toward the other car, then turned around and left. Based on these actions, he's also charged with hit-and-run driving and careless operation of a vehicle.

Hours later, when Coach Haslett finds out what his player has done, the player that he personally brought to the team, he must make a decision. His decision will affect his team as a whole and many as individuals, including on a very practical level, Pete Destefano. Perry plays Pete's position. You, the writer, wonder about this decision maker, and you ask yourself who is this person. Who is Jim Haslett?

Firsthand, you don't know who he is, and you won't know. Your repeated requests to the media police to interview him one-on-one have been unheeded. About a week from today, they'll finally produce him. Haslett will tell you that you have 10 minutes. You can only cover so much in 10 minutes, especially when you're primarily concerned about what he thinks about eight of his players. Other than talking to him about this whole roster-making process, you learn that he will start most days with a weight lifting workout at 5:30 a.m. and end many with another workout at midnight. It's obvious he's dedicated and hardworking, but almost all NFL coaches are.

Of course, this isn't his story. He's only relevant as to how he affects the undrafted rookies and the telling of their story. As to the telling, his media access rules have already been noted. As to the players, they seem to like him. "Haz is down," says Desmond Gibson. He's down. He's cool. He's consistent. He understands because he played. He doesn't motivate with rah-rah pep talks. He simply prepares his team. This is what you hear.

Then, there's what you read. Haslett is, according to what he a told the *Times-Picayune* in a July 15, 2000 article, a self-described "vacuum freak." "I like things to be neat," he said. "I'll vacuum the rug five times a day if I'm home. Sometimes I have to vacuum the bedroom before I go to sleep."

In the same article, Haslett said, "I don't do anything spur of the moment. I don't do spur-of-the moment things." He also said that he was impatient, but when patiently watching an emotional movie, he cries. "I couldn't stop crying watching 'Father of the Bride,'" he said.

The impatient, movie-crying man who loves to vacuum but hates spontaneity was born in Pittsburgh on December 9, 1955. He grew up in a blue-collar setting as the son of the owner of a window-washing business. After graduating from high school, he walked-on to the football team at a small school called Indiana University of Pennsylvania, where he became a standout defensive lineman, and where he would earn a degree in elementary education. By his senior year, he was too good a football player to have to teach tots for a living. The Buffalo Bills took him in the second round, converted him to a linebacker, and watched him flourish and make the 1980 and 1981 Pro Bowls.

In college and as a young pro, Haslett was a longhaired hell-raiser, but as he got older, he settled down. He married and started a family of two daughters and one son. His family became his only real hobby. His wife and kids and football are his life.

Immediately after retiring as a player in 1987, Haslett started coaching. First at the University of Buffalo, then in the World League, then back into the NFL as a linebacker coach for the Raiders. Before landing in New Orleans as a head man, he landed here as a defensive coordinator under Jim Mora in '95-'96, holding the same position for the Steelers from '97-'99.

The members of the New Orleans media who were here back in '95-'96 will tell you that Haslett has changed. Back in the mid-'90s, he was often "short" with the media. He could be intimidating. He sometimes used his blue eyes to stare right through a reporter. He was so intense at times that journalists joked that he was "psychotic."

Nowadays, while Haslett's intensity is still apparent, he isn't exactly wound as tight as a coat hanger in press conferences. When he's behind the microphone, he's fairly laid-back, witty, and can even be funny. He gets defensive at times, but that's to be expected of a rookie head coach. He's anything but "short." He doesn't leave until the reporters stop asking questions. Of course, this is only preseason, his first preseason as the head man. It's impossible to know how he'll handle a losing streak or a game lost on a blown call.

He's having to handle something right now. It's now Sunday night, and he's got to talk to the media about the Darren Perry situation. The situation is made more complicated by the fact that Perry is a repeat offender. On December 14, 1996 in Pittsburgh, when Perry was in his fifth season with the Steelers, he was involved in a strikingly similar incident. He allegedly rear-ended a vehicle at 2 a.m. causing slight injury to its driver, left the scene of the accident, and was later stopped and arrested on drunk driving charges. His blood-alcohol level was .15, .05 over the .10 Pennsylvania legal limit. Two months after the incident, Perry entered a plea bargain and paid a fine in restitution and was placed in a rehabilitative program.

So twice now, Perry has allegedly been too drunk to drive, caused an accident and fled the scene. When Haslett is asked how he will deal with the situation, he responds, "I'm going to let the courts deal with it on that end just like any other person, and the NFL will deal with it on the football end of it. I feel sorry for Darren. Obviously, he made a bad judgment. That's not like him. He's a good person. It's something he's going to have to live with. He's going to have to deal with it himself."

After Haslett responds to the next few questions, it's obvious that, while Perry, the courts, and the NFL will all eventually deal with the situation, Haslett will not. Perry will be on the practice field tomorrow running with the first team. He will also be the starter next week against Miami for the preseason finale, and he'll be the starter on opening day against Detroit. It will be as if nothing had ever happened.

When asked if Perry will be subject to team sanctions, Haslett says, "No. I think we'll deal with that once we see. I don't have a full understanding of what happened, to be honest with you. Just talking with him, there's more information that I want to get on it."

Whatever information Haslett has gathered or will gather doesn't stop him from playing Perry. It doesn't stop him from holding him out of even one practice. You wonder if Haslett would give an unheralded player the same treatment. You wonder if Haslett would've handled the situation differently if the free safety position hadn't already been weakened by the injury to Rob Kelly, leaving Perry as the only free safety with NFL experience. Finally, you wonder if Haslett's wife and kids had been the ones rear-ended or if he himself had been victimized by the cowardly action, would he still handle this matter the same way?

If you're an undrafted rookie, you're definitely wondering about this mess, about what will come of it. Perry is a likeable teammate. He seems like a good guy, but he's done some questionable things. When Perry says in a press conference that the incident will "make this team a stronger person," you don't know what he's talking about. In fact, it's a little sobering for you to see that Darren Perry is not being held accountable probably because he's Darren Perry. You know that if you don't perform to Haslett's liking, if you do anything that rubs him the wrong way, be it drunken hit-and-run driving or anything else, you will be held accountable. You will be released.

~

Monday, August 14, 2000, 5:05 p.m.

Rain is gushing downward. It is soaking everyone and everything on the practice field. It spares no one, not even the team's front office leader. Randy Mueller, however, isn't budging. He stands there without an umbrella, a hood, or at hat. He doesn't even wipe the rain from his eyes. He just watches, knowing that within two weeks he will have to cut almost three-dozen of the waterlogged players that he's observing. At present, his hair may be a wet mop, but underneath it, his mind is churning. His mere presence out here shows his dedication to either making what he believes to be the right personnel decisions or to showing his squadron he can handle the pouring rain.

At the end of the session, the players run wind sprints. They are blurred by the wall of water. Many of them are actually smiling. It makes sense. With the rain showering down in wheelbarrows, it is camp's coolest moment.

After practice, the players walk into the dining room knowing their last meal as a Saint could come at any time. The deadline for the first cut is eight days away, but the Saints could start cutting at any second. Shayne Graham knows that in all probability, he will be cut. "Honestly, I'm not nervous about the cuts because I want to play *now*," he says. "And if this isn't the place to do it, I need to get cut so I can go somewhere else."

Most of the undrafted rookies, however, want the extra practice time to prove themselves. "The next day's another day," says Jamal Brooks. Jamal thinks he has proved that he deserves to make it past this first cut, to be around for that Miami game, where he'll most certainly play a lot.

Jamal's plight is made more difficult by the fact that the Saints will probably only keep six or seven linebackers, and five of the spots are locked up. When linebacker coach John Bunting is asked about Jamal's chances, he responds, "Right now, the backup linebacker positions are way up for grabs."

"Ya'll are not settled with that at all?"

"Not at all. Not at all. So it's going to be really interesting what happens over the next two weeks."

"Hopefully, he's (Jamal's) going to have those two weeks to—"

"Oh, he'll get all those two weeks," says Bunting. "He'll get 'em."

Bunting seems like a sincere, straight shooter. He doesn't appear to be the type to blow a little feel-good sunshine. Sure, he doesn't have the final word, but there was a certain gleam in his eye when he said, "Oh, he'll get all those two weeks." It really gives one reason to believe that Jamal will get those two weeks, that he will make it past that first cut and have a chance to lay it all on the line against the Dolphins.

The Dolphins are presently not on Chase Raynock's mind. His right knee is. "It's sore right now," he says. "It's still not good enough to do anything right now. I'm still gonna be sitting for awhile."

Chase is off crutches and is working out on the exercise bike during practice. He doesn't consider this period to be a break. "I hate treatment. I'd rather be out there practicing." Instead of doing lineman drills, he's doing lots of knee extensions and other laborious exercises with the trainers.

As he bends to adjust his knee brace, he says that he's not going to think about how this injury will affect his attempt to make the team. "They've seen what I can do so far. I think by now they pretty much have a pretty good idea of what's going on."

In Chase's case, they do have a good idea, and it's good for Chase. Haslett will say tomorrow, "Chase Raynock is a guy we'll probably keep around on the practice squad."

Of course, even when the head man speaks, there are no guarantees. If Chase has not recovered by the final cut, the Saints could talk him into an injury settlement and release him. He knows this. He knows the team can't let an injured undrafted rookie take a roster spot, even if it's just a strain. So heal he must.

All the undrafted rookies know they now must make every rep as spectacular as possible. They've known that since day one, but this sense of urgency is very palpable now. The first big cut is circling them like condors. When Robert Brannon is asked if he's thinking about the cuts, he says, "I don't know. I don't know. I'm just taking it in." He pauses. "I don't really feel like talking about it right now."

No player sitting on the bubble wants to talk about it, much less think about it, including the older heads who are still trying to latch on permanently with a team. Look at wide receiver Ryan Thelwell. The Saints are his sixth team in just over two NFL seasons. Nothing about this slender, friendly native of London, Ontario seems like a football player until he starts running routes and catching passes. Despite his NFL skills, he can't seem to stick with an NFL team.

After being drafted out of the University of Minnesota in the seventh round in 1998 by the San Francisco 49ers, he lasted until the final cut. He knew going in that he wasn't likely to make it in a receiver corps led by Jerry Rice, Terrell Owens, and J.J. Stokes. So when San Diego signed him immediately to their practice squad, he felt fortunate. The Chargers eventually activated him, and he started three games and caught 16 passes, including one for a touchdown. Then, in the 1999 preseason, things in San Diego fell apart, and he was released on September 4, 1999. "I just didn't have a very good camp," he says.

Three days later, Seattle signed Thelwell to its practice squad, then released him in midseason. Two weeks after the Seahawks let him go, Jacksonville signed him to its practice squad, and two weeks after he first put on a Jaguars uniform, Pittsburgh signed him to its active roster. While Thelwell was flying from the Northwest to the Southeast to the Northeast, his truck and most of his belongings were still in Seattle. After the season, he flew back to Seattle and moved his possessions across the country to Pittsburgh, where he rented an apartment. Two months after settling into Steeltown, the Steelers waived him.

Then, six days later, before Thelwell could even look at a road map, the Saints inked him to a free agent contract. After the signing, he had thoughts of quitting, but after speaking to family and friends, he decided to move to New Orleans, and his girlfriend later joined him there. "I put in a lot of driving. I seen a lotta countryside," he says. "At least I've gotten to see a lot of good cities, you know, nice cities and play with a lot of good players and pick up a little bit from each player."

Thelwell says he knows he could perform better if he wasn't constantly in danger of having to change zip codes. "Security helps a lot," he says more than once. As to what keeps him going, he says, "I love playing the game." But there's also the practical motivation. He'd like to string together enough game checks to make more than the approximately $60,000 per year he's topped out at in his first two seasons of bouncing around. He'd like to buy a house and put some money away.

So here he is, literally sweating it out again. He's already taken the needle for dehydration and put up with other hardships for another shot. So far, he's discouraged by his failure to play in the Minnesota and Indianapolis games, but he's encouraged, even though he won't say it, by the generally poor receiver play in camp. "You just gotta keep going and pray and hope that one day it will work out."

The big positive to Thelwell's odyssey is that it shows that for some, there are second, third, fourth, fifth, and sixth chances. The negative is the realization that once you sign your first NFL contract, you become a commodity that can be bought and sold, traded and discarded.

Thelwell's six-team journey, however, is the furthest thing from the undrafted rookies' minds as they bed down for the night. They're doing everything in their power to focus on tomorrow's final two-a-day practice. They know they must impress someone somewhere in this league to make it on that first team, preferably this team.

Pete Destefano would prefer a lot of things right now. He'd prefer to be able to ease into sleep without battling congestion and other flu symptoms. He'd prefer not to have busted his nose open three times to the point of where he knows that if he really lays into someone, he'll bust it open again. Of course, he's not supposed to really lay into anyone at practice anyway, even though he'd prefer to, busted nose or not. Lastly, he'd prefer if Venturi would quit focusing on Eric Johnson in meetings and start paying attention to him. Yes, he knows that the NFL is not about what he prefers, but he prefers that it was.

~

Tuesday, August 15, 2000, 9:35 a.m.

Thick slops of mud have gathered all around the practice field. The playing surface, though, is, much to the players' disgust, very playable. It's as muggy as ever, and the players are having a hard time just breathing out in this bubbling gumbo.

Not giving an inch, the coaches begin to pepper the air with motivation.

"What the fuck's going on here?" shouts offensive coordinator Mike McCarthy. "Catch the ball and finish!"

"The ball, Darren, run to the fucking ball!" yells Haslett.

The hot tempers trickle down from the coaches to the coached. In lineman one-on-one drills, offensive tackle Jay Hagood grabs defensive end Bobby Setzer by the jersey and drags him to the ground. Setzer shoves him, but Hagood walks away. On the second go-round, after they lock up and separate, Setzer starts swinging. These aren't pushes, but real haymakers. Their fellow linemen egg them on. Some are laughing. Setzer wants to keep duking, but Hagood wants no part of it.

D.J. Cooper runs over toward Setzer, yelling, "Aaaaa!" in excitement. He gives his fellow defensive lineman a bear hug. "Yeah, Bobby Setzer!!"

Coop would say later, "I like to see a good fight. That's my boy right there, and I want to stick up for him." This is the Coop of the final minicamp, the one who stuck up for his fellow defensive linemen by getting in two fights in one day with the offensive line. This is the Coop whose favorite book and favorite movie is *The Outsiders*.

However, this hasn't been a territory-staking, Outsiders-type camp. After practice, Setzer would downplay the scrap. "We've been looking at each other for the last month, and things happen," says Setzer.

Something else is happening in lineman one-on-one drills. It's the education of Robert Brannon. Robert used to be solely a Brahman bull charging dead into the block and bashing it back. Now he's a shifty bull shark, showing off new rip, swim, and spin moves. Judging by his new techniques, he seems to have the desire to learn. If the Saints don't keep him, he needs to find another team or another league to continue to sculpt his talent.

At 10:50 a.m., Haslett stops the action and calls his soldiers into a huddle. This will mean only an hour and 50 minute practice. The players look relieved as they jog toward their tall leader. When they get there, however, they discover it's not over. In fact, it wouldn't be over for another 35 minutes.

During this period, one man becomes more visible. He's pacing up and down the sidelines, swinging a stopwatch. He picks up his cell phone, talks, puts it down, picks it up again. He's a relatively short man, but he's growing by the day. Soon, he will be taller and bigger and more evil than Darth Vader. Already, though, he's a dark force. Already, he can't be ignored. Already, he's the Turk.

Tonight, at the final night practice, the Turk will howl under the same full moon that appeared at the first night practice. What the moon means, only tomorrow will tell.

/ FIFTEEN /

TICK, TURK, TICK, TURK

WEDNESDAY, AUGUST 16, 2000, 6:30 A.M.

The air horn is filling the halls of Ellender Dormitory for the last time. For D.J. Cooper, it's waking him up to a reality that has nothing to do with football. Today, he must fly to Buffalo to face another personal tragedy. Last night, he learned that his wife Stacy's 32-year-old sister, Sandra, passed away. She left a husband and five kids. Now, Coop can't get to his wife fast enough. It's not fair, what's happening to her. Just last year, she lost her mother. Coop can relate to what she's feeling, to what many of them are feeling over the loss; he can relate too well. He's stared into caskets and seen the faces of loved ones. He's done it too many times for a man who's only 24 years old. These memories will flash over the next two days. He knows that. He knows he'll think about his mother, and about how her leaving this world made him grow up so fast. But now, he's trying to cast the memories aside, put football on hold and get to Buffalo, get to his wife.

~

When the 3 p.m. practice begins, it's just like any other one out here on the griddle. It doesn't feel like a ceremonious last practice. As the first team goes through its walk through, I realize everything I see from now until the last tick of the Turk will be colored by my long-awaited one-on-one interview with Haslett yesterday.

Haslett had just walked away from a session of posing for a picture with Randy Mueller. The photographer was forcing them to do goofy stuff like putting a hand on one another's shoulder. After Haslett moved away from the lens, we walked over to a corner of the media room, and he asked me what my book was about again, and when I told him, he asked, "Who's left?"

When I started to tell him, he started shaking his head for the first couple of names that I rattled off. As I continued to list the names, he stopped the head shaking, but the gist of what he said about each of them didn't give me the most confidence in the world. I now only see the door really open for two or three of them. He did say that the people who survive the first cut will play a lot against Miami. "So whoever's left will have a good shot at making this team," he said. He said how they perform in the Miami game will weigh about 80-85% in the decision as to whether they make the team. By that point theoretically, they'll have learned what they need to know, and they'll have plenty of opportunity to "just play."

I also asked him how much a player being drafted weighed in whether the team keeps that player. He responded, "It doesn't weigh anything. We'll put the best players on the field. Usually, if they're drafted, they're drafted for a reason. They're pretty good football players. But there are a lot of guys that will go unnoticed and get through the cracks. There's always one or two a year that make your team as undrafted players."

Contrary to what Haslett said, a player being drafted weighs a lot in a team's decision on whether to keep that player. He knows it. Mueller knows it. The drafted and the undrafted know it. Everyone in the NFL knows it. "It doesn't weigh anything"—that statement isn't true and can't be true. There's just too much money, reputation, and ego that goes into each draft pick.

Right now, the drafted and the undrafted are slugging it out on the dream fields for one last time. The action is remarkably crisp. It must be easier knowing it's the final day, knowing from tonight on, their lives won't be so tightly controlled.

The practice concludes by the offense taking on the defense in a kicking contest. The defense selects Doug Brien and the offense Shayne Graham. Each side douses the opposing kicker with water and jeers, making each kick an onerous one. Whoever misses first loses, and in this case, it's, ironically, Brien. In their lone real head-to-head, Shayne wins, even though he'll certainly be the one to lose his roster spot.

As the final horn sounds and the gleeful players almost skip off the field, some are singing. As wide receiver Joe Horn merrily chants, "Thibodaux, Thiii-bodaux," Ricky Williams is as quiet as Ricky Williams. He has slipped on a number "70" jersey, and his camouflage fools the fans. He makes it to the locker room without an autograph request. Toward the back of the pack, Coach Al Everest belts, "We love ya, Thibodaux!" The players mostly love that they're leaving.

Everything is leaving. The corporate tents are being dismantled; their air-conditioned coils are being rolled away. The game tents are already gone. In a few hours, the herd of Kawasaki Mules will back into a trailer, sputter to a stop and return to their home in Houma. For almost everyone involved, there's a sense of completeness.

But if you're a player without a guaranteed spot on the roster, one moving from a Thibodaux dorm to a Kenner hotel, your mission is far from over. You aren't close to being settled. Jamal Brooks puts the feeling into words, "You really don't know where you're at. There's been stories I've heard of people who you knew was gonna make it, who don't make it. People that you don't think's gonna make it, make it. It's the doubt. You not knowing, 'Am I gonna make it?'"

∼

Thursday, August 17, 2000, 5:00 p.m.

The NFL has left, but the dream hasn't died here. It's still growing. The men out there reaching toward their goals are now wearing a brilliant bright red. Watching the Nicholls State Colonels practice is a peaceful experience. It starts with there being no barriers to entry on Acadia Drive. You can simply pull up right next to the field and park in the shade. Other than a handful of onlookers, it's just you. You can get as close to the action as you want, with no one following you around, threatening to admonish you at every turn. Somehow, the Nicholls coaches are confident that you won't run onto the field and drag their quarterback down by his face mask.

Out here, the colors are so sharp. The field seems greener, the lines seem whiter, the oaks' bark seems blacker. The red on the Colonels' jerseys is clear and clean. There is nothing, no yellow ropes or anything else, to mess with the aesthetics of this place. It's as it was in the beginning, even better.

This is all a great gift to the Colonels and their 36-year-old head coach Daryl Daye, who is currently huddling his team, telling them to take care of their newly renovated locker room. In observing some of the Saints' practices, Daye fully understands the opportunity that each Saints hopeful has. He's dreamed their dream many times.

"It's kinda interesting how it all unfolded for me," says Daye in his good ol' boy, north Louisiana drawl. "I can remember. I was about seven years old, and it was the first time I saw Archie Manning. He came to our high school and spoke."

Daye's eyes get shiny as he looks beyond the cane field to the cotton fields of his home and the day Mr. Saint showed up at the gym at Huntington High in Ferriday. Daye took a picture with his hero that day, got his name in the paper for asking Manning a question, and knew he would follow the quarterback's path. "I wore number '8' all of my junior high career until I had a high school coach come and say, 'You're either gonna play quarterback or linebacker.'"

Daye chose linebacker and seemed destined to follow in his father Donnie's footsteps by playing for LSU. During the fifth game of his senior year in high school, an LSU assistant coach was in the stands, ready to receive a commitment from Daye, but Daye blew out his knee during the game, and there went the scholarship. He decided to walk-on anyway.

"The dream can't stop dreaming," he says. "I knew it was gonna be rough. I was dragging a bad wheel. We had 14-15 inside linebacker walk-ons at two-a-days. We had over 45-50 (total) walk-ons. We had a thing we started called the 'Walk-off Wall.' When you quit or 'walked off,' they took the tape off your locker, and they put your name on the wall. That thing went up and down several times, and them are tall ceilings. It really became a challenge more mentally because you saw so many people give up and quit."

Daye stuck it out, earned a scholarship by his senior year and earned a reputation as an excellent special teams player. He kept playing despite suffering injuries that, in all, would require four surgeries on his right knee, one on his left knee and two hernia operations.

While his love of the game kept him going, it wouldn't be enough to take his young, battered body to the next level. "I had the same dream as all the youngsters did. I caught the winning touchdown and ran the winning Super Bowl run, made the big play, you know, all the things you do as a young kid growing up, dreaming about playing in the NFL and LSU first. But it didn't take that shape."

What was taking shape was something his LSU head coach could see, but he couldn't. "(Coaching) kind of turned into my dream because Bill Arnsparger basically asked me to stay on and coach as a student assistant. I asked him why he wanted me to, and he said, 'I think you'd make a heck of a coach because sometimes the worst players make the best coaches.'"

In trying to be the best coach for Nicholls State, Daye can't think about his ol' NFL dreams. He's too focused on turning around the abysmal program he inherited. He's too occupied with taking a team that went 1-10 in his first season and transforming them into a winner. He's too busy trying to raise the graduation rate and raise attendance to make a Nicholls game at least competitive with the 5,000-plus people that regularly showed up to watch the Saints' night practices. Lastly, he's too worried about boosting the morale of a team that has had to deal with the tragedy of three teammates dying accidentally in just one year's time.

"There's a lot more to life than football," he says. Yes, there is, but for now, football is Daryl Daye's life, and it's how he can affect the lives of many others on this campus.

All across Nicholls, the scene is changing, and the biggest sign of change is at Ellender Dormitory. At the moment, there's a long line of girls there, waiting to check in where the big boys have just checked out. Nicholls is returning to what it was all along—a university. It's higher education within striking distance of little towns like Montegut, Bayou L'Ourse, and Paradis. It's a fine college degree that is feasible for the promising sons and daughters of shrimpers, drillers, welders, and the many other trades that make up the mosaic of the bayou land. With or without the Saints, Nicholls will endure and thrive.

Nevertheless, Nicholls and Thibodaux would like to thrive with the NFL. They feel like they've earned it. They (along with God, dry weather, and weekly aerials bombs of insecticide) have kept the mosquitoes away. They (along with God and meteorological forces) have limited the monsoons to one.

Nicholls-Thibodaux even kept away the love bugs, which are just now starting to arrive. Really, the love bugs are a symbol. They are the black bugs that remain intertwined even as they perish against a car windshield. The love bugs are Nicholls-Thibodaux and the Saints stuck to each other as lifetime mates. It's all about love, money, and football. Amen, or so be it.

~

Friday, August 18, 2000, 1:30 p.m.

Airline Highway stretches and slimes from the Bonnet Carre Spillway to the swamp to the modern 'burbs of Kenner and Metairie, toward downtown New Orleans. It is a mostly seedy strip, populated by some of the cheesiest, raunchiest motels in all of Americana. In one of these five-star flats, televangelist Jimmy Swaggart was caught in a telegenic position with a prostitute, then later proclaimed, "I have sinned."

Rising out of all the sin and skanky muck of Airline is a sparkling expanse of sports utopia. The first sculpted mass of steel and concrete is Zephyr Field, a model for modern minor league baseball stadia. Next door is the Saints' 19-acre practice complex, with its soft emerald fields and a 43,000 square-foot office building. It is impressive infrastructure for a seasonal business.

This head shed is known as "The Facility," but a better name could be "The Compound." Hedges and a green tarp cover every possible hole in the fence surrounding the practice field. To get onto the field, one must traverse two security gates and the media police. During practice, the television videographers are allowed to shoot only during the warm-ups. Once the drills start, they must pick up their cameras. Even the quarterback-to-receiver passing drill is considered top secret. Heaven forbid the Detroit Lions be allowed to get a dub of a tape that reveals the arc on one of Jeff Blake's throws. It must be a classified arc.

This afternoon, one of the journalists comments he'd have more access to a Russian missile base.

Actually, some of these security issues make sense. First, the barriers to the compound are appropriate because of the fanatical fans and more importantly, the car thieves that live in nearby run-down neighborhoods. The players wouldn't want their Hummers, Jags, and fancy SUVs exposed to the people who give Bunche Village a bad name. Bunche Village is just down Airline from the compound, and despite its quaint welcome sign, it's not exactly Mayberry.

There's nothing Barney Fife about practice today. It's all business and ultra precise. The Saints have been game-planning all week for their opening day opponent, and now, it seems as if it's all Lions. You get the feeling by the third team's decreased reps that the first cut has already been decided, even though it won't become official until Monday or Tuesday.

Strategically, if a player is going to be cut next week, he's better off being cut today so he can stand out on the waiver wire instead of being buried when teams start releasing players en masse over the weekend. The other side of it is most of these guys won't exactly be leaving here and walking into a paycheck. Every dollar they earn will help ease the transition to unemployment. When faced with this issue, most don't really know what they'd prefer, and because it's out of their control, they don't worry about it. The impending first big cut gives them all the worry they can handle.

The two positives for the undrafted rookies are, one, they've proved that they can make it through an NFL training camp, and, two, they're not there anymore. "It's nice to be back here and not in Thibodaux looking at them sugarcane fields," says Desmond Gibson, who is now shacking up with his fellow undrafted rookies at the nearby Wingate Inn. "You get your freedom back. It's not like you're a little kid anymore, getting checked in for bed and tucked in and stuff."

It's an odd feeling for Desmond and some of his teammates. After having attended a "Welcome Home" luncheon at the Hyatt Regency yesterday, they feel like they're part of the team, but even as they travel together for the final time tomorrow to a promotional practice in Mobile, Alabama, they know they're not really a Saint, not yet at least.

~

Saturday, August 19, 2000, 12:30 p.m.

No Saint player or coach wants to be here. The last thing the players want to do is put their huge bodies on a bus for two hours and 15 minutes, practice for two hours and then bus the same distance back home. But this is part of how a millionaire is made, by doing inconvenient promotional stuff, by sacrificing your free will in the name of hype. So as the buses exit the I-10 and drive through some Mobile projects, the players must wipe the grimaces from their faces and march mightily into Ladd-Peebles Stadium.

For some, this may not seem like the place to be today. But for one week, it is the place to be in the NFL. This is the site of the Senior Bowl, the nation's most prestigious collegiate all-star game. It draws almost every NFL coach, scout, major agent, and beat writer. They come with their stopwatches and notebooks and their eagle eyes. They watch practice and watch more practice, and they silently Ooo and Ahh, and they not so silently gab at the bar of the Adams Mark Hotel. Senior Bowl week is where draft stock goes up or down, and careers begin and end.

What's going on out here today has got nothing to do with anyone's career, except those Mobileans affiliated with trying to convince the Saints to move their training camp to the Port City. To help generate the publicity, vendors are selling "Camp Mobile 2000" shirts and hats, as if a one-day publicity practice constitutes a full training camp.

Mobile is doing their best to put on a show in conditions no less humid than those in Thibodaux. A couple hours ago, the Saintsations played a flag football game against members of the Mobile media and some local dignitaries. The Saintsations showed deceptive speed and not so deceptive ability to make the defense stare en route to a 35-7 victory. The Saintsations did, however, benefit from field position near their opponents' goal line and from penalties levied against their competitors for "immoral thoughts."

As practice gets ready to begin, one realizes this isn't just any practice. It can't be when public officials are presenting all the key Saints people with keys to the city. Then, a local trumpeter horns out the National Anthem, which is followed by a procession of 40 girls dressed in colorful petticoats, pastel dresses, lined up along the sideline, holding their parasols. These darlings are called the "Azalea Trail Maids." Despite sweating as much as football players in full pads, the Trail Maids smile and maintain their poise. Just before practice "kicks off," there's a flyby by a military plane of some kind. I think the announcer says, "Coast Guard." It doesn't make much noise, and it's late. A timely F-16 buzz, it ain't.

If all that wasn't enough, we soon find out that there will be a PA announcer calling out the drills. He announces authoritatively, "In a minute, the first practice session will begin. It will involve the quarterback-center exchange." As the fans hunch forward anticipating the drama of the quarterback placing his hands under the center's crotch, the PA announcer appeases them by announcing, "The drill will start momentarily."

Momentarily, the 5,000 fans scattered throughout the 40,000-seat stadium will see their Saints. But we'd rather see the Saintsations take on the Azalea Trail Maids. It would be a pom-poms versus parasols free-for-all. Petticoats would fly and halter-tops would barely hold on. It would be the Old South versus the New Woman, Genteel Mobile versus Flashy Metairie. The prospect of a rematch, especially a muddy rematch, might just be the gimmick Mobile needs to get training camp next year.

Next year, though, is a universe away for the Saints' undrafted rookies. For now, they can innocently stare at the Saintsations in the postpractice food tent. They can whoop it up tonight on the town. Sunday will be theirs, too. But come Monday or Tuesday, they'll be talking turkey and talking Turk.

∾

Monday, August 21, 2000, 3:05 p.m.

A ball is tipped into the air above the practice field at the Saints' Metairie compound. Pete Destefano lunges for it. He is diving like a center fielder with his body parallel to the ground and his arms outstretched. He feels the leather touch the tips of his fingertips, and he rocks it back into the cradle of his hands. He makes the interception no more than a few millimeters above the grass. He truly gave his all on this play, throwing every ounce of himself out there, even though he knows he's already been cut.

Pete knows what no other player knows because he saw the list Coach Venturi left on the table earlier that day in the d-backs meeting. After glancing at it, he had no trouble understanding the bottom line.

After practice, Pete wishes the Saints would just make it official, even though he hopes he's got the wrong information. "How long are they gonna string this thing out?" he asks.

Haslett said in Mobile they'd probably start making the cuts today. They haven't, meaning all 12 cuts will come tomorrow, and everyone in this locker room can feel it coming. I approach the side-by-side lockers of D.J. Cooper and Desmond Gibson.

"Talk to me tomorrow," says Coop, who's visibly nervous.

"What do you know?" asks Desmond.

"Nothing," I half lie and half tell the truth. Based on what I've heard, I think he will be cut, but I'm not going to dampen his spirits by telling him this. Certainly, no one has come out and told me definitively that he will be cut, if there is such a thing as a definitive statement in this league. As the history of this camp has proved, I know very little about what will happen.

"Well, it's in God's hands now," says Desmond.

"Yeah, God, Randy Mueller, and Jim Haslett."

"God can affect them, too."

At this point, he can only hope so.

/ SIXTEEN /

THE TURK STRIKES TWELVE

TUESDAY, AUGUST 22, 2000, 6:15 A.M.

As the undrafted rookies wake up this morning at the Wingate Inn, they rise to a sky full of mixed colors and mixed signals. It has rained and rained hard. The roads are still slick and gray. The dawn is still broken up by purple clouds. One way or the other, fate will attack.

From 7 a.m. to 9 a.m., the players begin to make their way through the door of the Saints' compound. Surely, they know by now that the Turk will be waiting. He is. He clips them as they come through. His weapons are his iceberg eyes. If he makes eye contact, he has them. They are in his grip, capable of only marching upstairs to Haslett's office to hear what, at best, can be a brief explanation for their release and in any event will only prolong a miserable day.

Some will make it through the first door. Somehow they will get past the Turk. But later, he will find them. He will comb the locker room, seek them out and snare them with his stare.

While the turking is taking place inside the compound, a handful of media members are gathered outside the fence. Two media policemen are across the chain-links from us, warning us that we can't interview released players on the grounds of the compound. Sometime around 9 a.m., Jamal Brooks leaves the building and goes toward his car. He looks at me, and I give him the thumbs-up signal. I think it's safe to do this because of what his position coach has told me, '*Oh, he'll get all those two weeks.*' Jamal doesn't return my thumbs-up signal. He shakes his head and says, "Nah, man, they..." His voice trails off. "I'll talk to you about it later."

The reality and the humanity of what is happening hits me like it won't again. My gut gets suddenly hollow. Jamal has never showed disappointment until now, when he just can't help it. He's only visibly down for a few seconds, then he rights himself. But inside, it's got to be tearing him up.

A few minutes later, the Turk pops his head out of the player door, looks left, then right and pops back inside. A minute later, two vans shoot out from behind the back of the building. They are filled with large men. Obviously, these are the released players. I hustle off to my truck to follow them as they leave the compound.

Where they're heading makes no sense. They're bustling down Earhart Expressway toward downtown. The hotel is in the other direction. At first, it seems as if they'll get off at an exit and stop at a medical facility for a physical. But they don't get off. They follow the expressway until it stops, then turn right on Carrollton and head into Uptown. After they go left on Claiborne, I'm really confused. Are they taking them to the Superdome to see what they will miss? Eventually, they turn right on Napoleon and stop in the parking lot of a medical complex. It sure is a far-flung physical. Even if it is the office of the team doctor, Tim Finney, one has to wonder why the Saints didn't just bring him to the compound.

When the players start getting out of the car, I'm hoping I'll stop seeing familiar faces, but that doesn't happen. Cut are 12 in all, and the following six of ours: Robert Brannon, Desmond Gibson, Shayne Graham, Bill LaFleur, Pete Destefano and Jamal Brooks.

When Jamal sees me, he has a worried look on his face. "What about the book?" he says. "Is anybody left?"

His career is in jeopardy, and he's expressing concern about my book. I tell him that Coop and Chase are still around.

When the group settles into chairs in the doctor's waiting room, they're rapping about last night's Monday night game and their ex-teammate K.D. Williams making a few plays for the Packers. This bunch looks different than Amp Campbell or Terrence Miles looked after they were cut. It's because they're together, talking about anything but whatever it is they're feeling inside. No one is allowed to let it down yet, but two are doing it anyway.

Robert Brannon has his bucket hat pulled low over his eyes. When I talk to him, he keeps saying, "It's gonna be okay. It's gonna be okay." His fellow defensive lineman Winfield Garnett looks much worse. This is Garnett's third unsuccessful attempt at sticking with an NFL team. Despite being a former cocaptain at mighty Ohio State, he's failed to make it to opening day with the Jaguars, the Seahawks, and the Saints. He's now staring into space, saying nothing, staying in oblivion. He seems like he sees the end of his pro football road.

After a few minutes, it becomes obvious that the players will have to wait awhile in this crowded office. They will be called up individually, sporadically. "This is bullshit," says Desmond Gibson, echoing the sentiments of everyone. They're all worried about missing their planes. They would have signed anything the Saints wanted them to sign so they could get out of there and put the compound and the *fleur-de-lis* in the rearview mirror, just so they could be on a plane soaring over Lake Pontchartrain toward home.

They're trying their best to keep their mind off the obvious. Some try to joke. Others cell-phone their agent or their parents or their girlfriends.

Shayne Graham seems very loose for just having been cut. "I'm disappointed, but, I mean, I've known for a while now that this was gonna happen," he admits.

For Pete Destefano, this moment is especially low. He looks at a few of the players in the room, and he frankly can't believe he's as bad as some of them are. Trying to find a positive, Pete is pleased that Coach Venturi told him that the Jets showed some interest in him. So now he's talking to Bill LaFleur about suiting up for New York, about playing along side Scott Frost, Bill's teammate at Nebraska. Pete says it would be great to be in New York City. "They treat Italians like kings there," he says.

Sitting next to Pete, Bill LaFleur says he knew from the beginning he had no chance of making the team outside of an injury to Toby Gowin. But he adds, "I owe the Saints a lot." He says Haslett told him the Bears are interested in him. While Chicago with its swirling winds isn't the best place for a punter, he says, "Anywhere's better than nowhere."

Anywhere in the NFL is where Jamal Brooks would like to be, and he is thinking deeply about where he might end up. "I'm more curious to see what happens. I'm disappointed because it didn't happen like I wanted it to happen, but there's been a lot of stuff in my life that happened like that, but then in the long run it ended up being positive. Just like sitting out a year, but I ended up going to the Saints. I'm just curious to see what I'm 'posed to learn from this, what I'm 'posed to get out of this."

Across the room, Desmond Gibson looks over at rookie quarterback Marc Bulger. The two played high school ball against each other in Pittsburgh. Desmond tells him, "Everybody in the 'Burgh's gonna be asking questions. I sure ain't looking forward to that."

Desmond and the others are really looking forward to getting the hell out of this doctor's waiting room, where they will wait an hour and a half. They will then be transported back to the compound, which is the last place they want to see, to get their flight itineraries and any personals left in their lockers. Not until 12:15 will they all be back at the hotel, packing for their afternoon flights.

Most of the undrafted rookies have been asked by Haslett if they would consider coming back to the practice squad, and they all obviously said, "Yes." While the practice squad isn't the roster, the pay isn't bad at about $4,000 per week, and the education is priceless. Further, there's always the chance the Saints or any other team in the league will activate them. This "activation" can happen at any time by any team, and in addition to giving them a chance to play, being activated gives the player about an $8,000/week raise.

However, it's unlikely the Saints would release someone at the first cut and let them dangle on the waiver wire for a week if they intended to recall them. The practice squad talk was almost certainly a way for Haslett to put a positive spin on a very negative moment. Haslett also mentioned to some of them the possibility of playing in NFL Europe or other leagues to get experience. Pete speaks for some when he says he'll play in another league if that's what it takes, but he's leery about beating up his body for much less money when he has too much else going for him. Others, like Jamal, are ready to play in another league immediately, assuming the NFL is not a possibility.

Unlike some head coaches who have the Turk do all the work, Haslett decided that he should personally tell players why they were being released. "I just feel like, being an ex-player, that I should be the one that tells them why or why not," says Haslett.

Despite Haslett's benevolent intentions, when a player already knows what's coming, it's difficult to listen. "I didn't really pay attention," says Desmond. "I could tell it was rehearsed."

Desmond's right. Haslett's spiel probably was rehearsed. Haslett undoubtedly didn't know them well enough to say something touching and personal; consequently, it was going to come out a little wooden no matter how glib he tried to be. Moreover, Haslett is a rookie cutter. He hasn't talked the talk enough to be Clintonesque.

So while Desmond calls it correctly, Haslett also appears honest when he says, "It wasn't easy on me, either."

It wasn't easy because he's been near where they are. His being cut, as a veteran who no longer had what it took, was only part of his memory. The other images in his head were all those years he prospered but had to watch his friends get cut and watch people he'd just gotten to know get cut, and see people coming into camp on top of the world get cut.

Yet as a player, as an assistant coach, someone else was doing the cutting. Now, it's his call and Mueller's call. So when he takes a breath at the press conference and says, "It was pretty tough," he isn't just smoking sugarcane.

Back at the compound, the Turk is pleased that everything went off without a glitch. He sounds like an executioner who has been successfully lowering the guillotine all day. "From our standpoint, it went pretty well," says the Turk. "None of them reacted poorly to it," he adds, as if it's possible to have a reaction when your head is chopped off.

"You like to leave the players with a good impression," he says. "You don't want to let them think your organization doesn't know how they're handling it." It's important, he emphasizes, "that they leave with a good taste in their mouth."

A good taste in their mouths? The Turk couldn't leave them with a good taste in their mouths if he escorted them out the door with go-go girls, into a limousine with a hot tub adorned with champagne, cheeseburgers, and more go-go girls.

It was surprising to many that the Turk tagged Pete and Jamal this early. Eight days ago, Jamal's position coach, John Bunting, had said Jamal would make it past this cut. It's now obvious that he didn't have enough influence over the decision. I eventually ask Bunting, "So sometimes you may not get everything you want as a position coach?"

His response: "Oh, that's absolutely, that's more of the rule than the exception."

As to why Jamal didn't make the roster, he says, "We just felt like he wasn't far enough along to help us this year. To me, it was a difficult cut because the kid had really given everything he had, and he was making progress. I wish we had more time with him. Down the road we will get back in touch with Jamal Brooks. He's someone that I'd like to see get more experience in football, because he has good football instincts."

In Pete's case, Coach Venturi says, "He just really got caught in a numbers game." The Saints were going to keep four veteran safeties, and Venturi says ex-Canadian leaguer Gerald Vaughn will probably be the fifth because of his productivity in camp. Destefano's infamous misread during the night practice in the 9-on-7 drill was "a factor" in letting him go, "but not *the* factor." "Nothing boils down to that," says Venturi. "It's all a cumulative evaluation."

"I think he's a kid that can play in the National Football League. I think he's an ideal developmental guy. I'll be amazed if he isn't on a practice squad roster somewhere, whether he's on ours or not, I don't know, because we have so many numbers at defensive back because of the injury to Kelly and the injury to Fred Thomas."

With Pete leaving town, Chase Raynock will now have a hotel room to himself. "It's not the way you wanna get your own space," says Chase.

When Chase is asked what it's like seeing so many new friends leave, he repeatedly says that it's "part of the business," which shows he's already learned the company line. "It's part of the business," says Chase. "I mean you gotta learn to distance yourself from that. You can't feel emotion about that shit, or it's going to be eating at ya."

Chase has enough eating at him already with not being able to run on his knee. "Like I said before, I came here to play. I didn't come here to sit on the sideline, and that's what I'm doing right now." He doesn't think he'll play against Miami and can only hope the knee is healed enough for the team to recall him to the practice squad next week. "I'm just disappointed. I mean, I'm just distraught right now. It's hard to deal with, you know," he says. His face is red, and his voice is trailing some. He might cry if this discussion goes any further.

In another row of lockers, Coop looks relieved. "I'm just glad to say I'm still here," he says.

It's been a happy, but awkward day for Coop. It wasn't easy watching his roommate, Desmond Gibson, leave. "I really didn't want to say too much to him," says Coop. "It's kinda hard to say something, you know, because we're all playing for that spot. I can't really feel like he's feeling because I wasn't cut."

Coop says Clancy has told him the team will either keep him or his friend and fellow d-lineman, Bobby Setzer. It will depend on who performs the best against Miami. "Me and Setzer are close, you know, but I can't really worry about it, just like he really can't worry about it."

This is a surprise. Setzer is technically sound for a rookie, and he's got a great motor, but he appears to be smaller than Coop, even though Setzer's listed as 6-4, 280 and Coop's listed as 6-3, 283. The ex-Boise State Bronco is definitely not as athletic as Coop. As far as play-making ability goes, the nod again goes to Coop. Even though Setzer has made fewer mistakes than his linemate, Coop's got a lot more upside. Setzer's a nice guy, but this shouldn't be a contest. A contest, though, it is.

Friday night, Coop and Setzer will roam the Dome. The winner will get all the fortune and foam. The loser will go home.

/ SEVENTEEN /

HOME DOME

FRIDAY, AUGUST 25, 2000, 6:57 P.M.

The Louisiana Superdome is a universe, Coop's universe. It's a constellation of light and a galaxy of space—Coop's lights and Coop's space. It's the largest indoor stadium in the world, and its every bulb and brick belongs to Coop. It's Coop's coop. It has to be. It's the home of the Sugar Bowl, but it's all Cotton Bowl crunk tonight.

Last year's Cotton Bowl was the real Coop, MVP Coop: Throwing the whole o-line in the dumpster, sacking the Texas quarterback twice, stopping Longhorns three times behind the line of scrimmage, making a Horn victory impossible and a Hog victory probable. That's gotta be Coop tonight—blood-snorting, pig-suey-Razorback-whooping, Cotton Bowl, Coop.

Tonight, Coop's calling on more than Dallas crunk and Hog hops. He's looking through the roof, pointing up high. "I called everybody in my family and told them to pray for me," he says.

As Coop nearly implodes from all his crunk and gospel go, the Saints are bouncing up and down, preparing for kickoff. But many people are missing from the sideline. It's an empty feeling. You can't help but wonder what would happen if they had this opportunity.

Coop has it, and he feels it. He grabs Ricky Williams and shakes him, making his dreads flap, telling him, "We gotta get crunked!" He hops over to Pro Bowl defensive end Joe Johnson and gives him the same message.

During the Dolphins' first few offensive series, Coop watches his fellow rookie defensive end Darren Howard get manhandled by Dolphins rookie offensive tackle Todd Wade. Wade is sealing off Howard as effectively as the other offensive tackles who played against Howard in the preseason. In four preseason games, Howard will do next to nothing and finish with a whopping two tackles.

Despite all of the hoopla surrounding Howard, Coop is a better player. Down deep, he knows that he is, or at least, you hope that he knows it because it's true. "You know, Darren's a good player," says Coop. "(But) he really doesn't have a lot of stuff to learn and stuff. He's just gotta learn one position. He don't really gotta do too much special teams work. That's the good thing about being drafted high."

Being the number one pick of the Mueller-Haslett era means the table has been laid out for Howard, whom the team has handed a 1.43 million dollar signing bonus. He's getting to play his old college position and only that position. He's getting all the reps, coaching, and patience he needs to be Mueller-Haslett's marquee young player. Coop is not complaining about the team's special treatment toward Howard. He knows it's just the way things are. He knows that if he's going to make this team he'll have to cram into his head two positions and every special team unit. He'll have to know their every nuance and make it all look easy out on the field.

Even though Coop has more responsibilities than any other d-lineman, he's still managed to outplay his fellow rook. While many may argue that Coop has faced second- and third-teamers, and Howard's had to battle against the first team, the bottom line is that when the lights are on, Coop has made plays, and Howard hasn't. Moreover, Coop has done things in practice, like his first night practice pile-drive of Willie Roaf, that Howard has not come close to doing.

Be all that as it may, Howard will probably play fairly well this year. He will get the sacks and get the big stops that he's not getting now because teams will game plan like they're not game planning now. And their plan will be to focus on Howard's studhorse veteran linemates, Norman Hand, La'Roi Glover, and Joe Johnson. The older heads will get all the double teams. They will get the attention, which means the rookie will get some nice table scraps.

This game, though, isn't about Howard, whose place is safe and

secure. It's about Coop, who's fighting for his family and won't get any
table scraps to feed them. At 9:15 to go in the first half, Coop finally
enters the ring. He's brought in on a goal line drill as an extra d-lineman.

The line bunches together, digs into the turf. The ball snaps. Coop
holds his block. He thinks it's a stop. He's shaking his head. He's teasing
the running back. "You didn't make it. You didn't make it." Next thing
he knows the kick team is lining up. The Dolphins *did* score. He considers
bolting for the sideline but knows he won't make it in time. He's the
swing guy. He's not supposed to be there. The holder is counting out a
cadence. He hopes the refs don't see the 12 men on the field. The kick
goes through, the yellow hankie goes up. Aaaaaa!

Seconds later, Coop is trotting off the field into the flapping jaws
of Jim Haslett. Haslett calls him a "dumb ass." When he stops his
chewing, Coop sits on the bench and casts his head down. Setzer
comes over to console him. After his friend leaves, Coop won't raise
his head. "Dumb ass"—he knows he acted like one. Knows he
should've been paying attention. "Any time you get called a 'dumb ass'
it bothers you," he would say later.

Coop knows he has too much at stake here. He's got to raise his
head. He's got so much weighing on him. The bills. The tragedies. The
dream. It ain't easy coming in cold on goal line with all the Who Dats
screaming, and the lights blaring. Forget about it, he tells himself.
They made the extra point anyway. The penalty has nothing to do with
the score of the game. The head comes up. He'll have to wait through
halftime to get another chance.

The second half starts. The Dolphins have the ball. The Saints'
second team D is in, but not Coop. He's bopping. He can't wait to go
in there and erase the 12 men, to turn the yellow flag into a sack. But
when the Dolphins begin their second drive of the half, he's still not in.

With 3:24 to go in the third quarter, he's in. He's in. He's in his
stance, and he can hardly contain himself.

The series goes three and out. The action goes away from him
each time. On one play, he drops back into coverage. Nothing really
happens. He's happy for the stop, but itching to get dirty.

After a fumbled punt return, he's back! The fumble's bad for the
team, but this isn't about team, it's about him, and it's damn good for
him. The Dolphins have got the ball in the red zone, and on the second

play, they run right at Coop. Coop throws off his block and stops the tailback, holding him to a three-yard gain, forcing a third and goal from the five-yard line.

Coop is starting to feel it, and he tells the offensive tackle, "You can't hold me. You're a second-teamer. I'm gonna be a Pro Bowler one day."

On the next play, the Dolphins throw a quick pass and score. The score isn't good, but the extra plays were. The tackle was. Coop's loose. He's warm. He's got a whole freaking quarter to go, and he's already warm.

Now, it's a TV timeout before the next series, and Coop is eyeing up Mike Quinn, the Dolphins backup quarterback. "Quinn. Quinn," he hollers. "I need a sack, man. I'm trying to make the team." Quinn grins.

On play one, Quinn takes the ball and hands off to Brian Edwards. The play goes left, away from Coop, and Coop chases it down, holding the runner to a three-yard gain. A few plays later, he chucks his blocker like a grocery sack and stops the runner for a one-yard gain. During the drive, Coop's confidence is visibly sprouting, taking him over. He's backing up the talk, busting up the blocks. The hesitation and thinking and the awe have gone away. It's all action and reaction. It's all instinct and agility. It's two assists on two more tackles this series and being part of a goal line stop inside the one-yard line.

Just as Coop and the boys save the day, they hand the offense a dilemma. A defensive goal line stand always turns into an offense's goal-line nightmare. But it's the kind of predicament somebody needs right now. A man of Coop's undrafted lineage is craving this very situation. His name is Jake Delhomme. Jake is one of the Saints' backup quarterbacks and a former rookie free agent. He's never made an opening day roster, and this is his fourth try. Tonight, he's gotta do something special, or his friend Billy Joe Tolliver will make the roster as the third quarterback, and Jake will be watching yet another opening day from his home in Breaux Bridge, Louisiana.

Thus far tonight, Jake has stepped backwards. He's had three drives, and two were three-and-out, and one ended with an interception. So as he stands here under center with his feet in his own end zone, he's got the chance for redemption, and he can redeem himself as Superman. He can throw aside all the frustrations that have mounted for the four years since he left Louisiana-Lafayette as the Ragin' Cajuns all-time passing leader.

And there certainly have been frustrations. After being cut during training camp as a rookie in 1997, he was told by Mike Ditka that the Saints would bring him back right away to the practice squad, but they didn't recall him for another three months. "I think I got a taste of the business right there," says Jake. "It's hard in this league to put total trust in someone."

Next, Jake put total trust in his abilities when he suited up for the World League in the summer of 1998. But he soon began to doubt himself when he couldn't even win the starting position in the football equivalent of the minor leagues. It would take another year before he realized his self-doubt was misplaced. "Lo and behold," he says, "the guy I was backing up was a guy by the name of Kurt Warner. And he wasn't that bad of a quarterback."

Kurt Warner! He *is* the dream. From stocking cereal boxes at the Hy-Vee to having his own cereal, Warner is an undrafted who has made the ultimate journey. And Warner wasn't the only Super Bowl-winning Ram to make it. The guy who snapped Warner the balls, Mark Gruttadauria, he made it, and the guy who gave Warner the field position, the 1999 NFL-leading kick returner, Tony Horne, he made it, too. So did the guys who stopped the other team so Warner could get the ball back—defensive lineman D'Marco Farr, buzz-bee linebacker London Fletcher, and Mike "The Tackle" Jones, who went from an unknown college running back to the linebacker that saved the Super Bowl. And don't forget the specialists, punter Rick Tuten and kicker Jeff Wilkins. All of them are world champions, and all of them began NFL life in the undrafted line.

So Jake and Coop and the rest know it can be done because it's just been done, and we're not just talking about making the roster, we're talking Pro Bowls, and that big grail that fulfills you like no other, the one that bears Lombardi's name and is as sterling as is the moment that is the Super Bowl. So when Jake backpedals into his end zone and pay dirt is 105 yards away, he remembers his podnah Kurt, the same Kurt who called him after he won last year's Dallas game in his first start. Jake lets that Dallas feeling fill his veins, imagines that he's eating some "Warner's Crunch Time" cereal and throws a bullet to Chad

Morton for 13 yards. And the rest is easy, or at least, he makes it look that way. 99.5 yards, 10 plays, two minutes, two seconds, one touchdown. Miami 22, NO 17.

Jake raises his arms, marches off the pitch, mythically passes that box of cereal to Coop, who's all full of undrafted Crunch and John Randle crunk. On the second play of the Miami drive, Coop shows that burst that no one can teach, the one the Saints better wise up and keep, and he gets into the backfield and trips the ballcarrier for a one yard loss. The Miami 'O' goes four and out and, back comes Jake to sprinkle a few more flakes of Undrafted Crunch Time magic.

This time Jake's got 50 seconds, 70 yards and no timeouts. And he makes it interesting. He squeezes in six plays and takes 'em to the Miami 23. The gun sounds, and the Saints don't score and don't win, but Jake Delhomme looks like he has.

And Coop should, too. Should. Won't find out until the weekend if his six-tackles-in-one-quarter-performance was enough to make the roster, or until next week if it's enough to make the practice squad. But right now, Coop's not thinking about that. He's out there slapping skin, making friends. "I'm a people person," he said once. "Anybody will tell you I get along with anybody." And anybody will, especially the dozens of Dolphins he's befriending right now. Some of them have never seen Coop until just this instant, and now they've known him forever.

In the locker room, Coop's all smiles and all slow to take the uniform off. "I got me some Miami stuff, boy!" he says as he takes a piece of fleece apparently from a Dolphins jersey that was stuck to his own jersey and puts it in a jar.

Coop's mood is nothing like after those other games when he was so worried about every little mental mistake, he couldn't see that he was competing in the league of all leagues. Now, he's felt the truth. "I just feel that I can play," he says. "I know that I can play in the N-F-L."

Teammate Marcus Price hears him and laughs. Price tells him, "You were cold out there tonight. *Cold!* You gonna be in the Pro Bowl one day."

Coop smiles and qualifies, "I ain't at the Randle status yet." He winks and thinks about his next move. "I can't wait to get on the phone so I can talk to my wife and friends because I had them all praying."

After tonight's performance, Coop shouldn't need any prayers to get on the team, but after talking to his position coach, it's hard to tell. Coach Clancy's eyes get real serious when I bring up Coop. "Yeah, Cooper did well, also Bobby Setzer did well," he says. He wasn't asked about Setzer.

"He made some plays," Clancy says about Coop. "He made some mistakes also so you know nobody had a perfect game. It was the same way with Bobby. He made some plays and had a couple of nice pass rushes, you know, it happens with young guys. So like I said, we gonna sit down as a staff, and nothing's been determined between neither one of those two young guys. We just gonna see what's happening and may the best man win."

Best man win? Who's zooming who? Setzer played solidly, but he didn't make any tackles. What's all this talk about Setzer? This is Coop's night. This is his dome.

~

Saturday, August 26, 2000, 11:10 a.m.

The Saints have said they're not cutting anyone until tomorrow, but something isn't right. My gut is telling me it might happen this morning. It's telling me not to trust what they've said. So I drive into the city. When I hit the Saints' compound, the media members tell me Haslett has canceled his 12:15 press conference. He's stood us all up.

Outside the media room, I notice that a player, who has likely been cut, carrying a garbage bag full of stuff to his car. I go back inside the media room and ask two media cops if the cuts are occurring. They say they know nothing about it. Maybe they don't, but when I go back out to the parking lot, another media cop sticks his head out of the player's door and looks both ways. It's as if he's making sure the coast is clear. The Saints aren't very good at deception.

A few minutes later, Coop appears in the parking lot. "Coop," I call out to him through the chain-links. "Everything cool?"

"Naw, man. I've been waived." He looks pretty calm. He's fixing to climb into Norman Hand's SUV.

"Damn, I'm sorry, man. Where you going?"

"I'm heading to the *casa*. I'm going home, man." There seems to be some relief in his words. It makes sense considering what his wife has had to contend with by herself the past six weeks.

Later, at the Wingate Inn, Coop talks about how the Turk picked him off while he was walking outside to do his conditioning. Coop was one of 17 players who were getting slashed. The Turk was staring people into submission one after the other.

The Turk had just been in the locker room, where he'd clipped off several Saints, as explained by placekicker Doug Brien in his August 28, 2000, entry in his diary on his web site, www.kicking.com:

> *All of a sudden a man, who at this time of the year is known as "the Grim Reaper," entered the locker room. He approached players and asked them to get their playbooks and go upstairs to talk to the head coach. I could feel the tension in the air. Most guys sat with their eyes fixed to the floor, praying that the Grim Reaper wasn't coming to visit them. This lasted for fifteen agonizing minutes as the Grim Reaper made his way around the locker room slashing and burning and crossing off names from his long list. It got so bad for Jason McEndoo that he asked the Grim Reaper twice if he needed to talk to the head coach. He was told "no" both times.*
>
> *When the Grim Reaper finished his work, those of us that remained went out to the field for conditioning. We all assumed that those of us on the field had made the team. In the middle of our grueling workout, I heard a player say, "If they cut me after making me do this conditioning, I am going to kick some ##?@!" It was kind of a joke because everyone out there thought they had made the team. However, that was not the case. On Sunday a few more cuts were made including Jason McEndoo and Billy Joe Tolliver. I guess the slash and burn isn't over until the 3 pm deadline officially hits.*
>
> *This year's was one of the toughest cuts I've witnessed. First, I have never been on a team that has worked so long and hard in the off-season; everyone attended two training (mini) camps and was in town throughout the off-season.*

Everyone released had worked so hard to be with the team.
Also, guys are usually pulled from meetings and told to talk
to the coach. That gives the player a little privacy in the
locker room to pack his belongings and leave. It also comes as
more of a surprise because no one knows when the cuts are
happening. This year everyone witnessed most of the cuts.
All we could do was sit and hope our number wasn't called;
it was agonizing.

Coop didn't think he would be in any agony, not after his performance last night. "I don't really know how to feel because everyone
on the team acted like they were so surprised I was getting cut. They
all tell me that I'm gonna be playing somewhere."

Somewhere may be with the Saints, he thinks, because Haslett
says he has a chance at being recalled for the practice squad. He says
Haslett kidded with him about the 12-man-on-the- field penalty. Coop
admitted to the head man that he'd made a "dumb ass" maneuver and
says he doesn't harbor any ill feelings about being called a "dumb ass."
"I like Coach Haslett," he says. "I think he's gonna be a real good coach
pretty soon."

At the moment, Coop is not a man who's broken up over being
cut. With the possibility of the practice squad, he's not sure enough
about his status to be emotional. More importantly, now that he's
flying back to Fayetteville, his mind is on something else. "I need to
be at home. I need to be around her (his wife) at least for a couple of
days. It was like a one-night thing when I went down there (to Buffalo
for his sister-in-law's funeral), and it's like I was gone the next day. I
need to be there and hold her and tell her everything's gonna be all
right. I know she wants to look in my eyes and see that everything's
gonna be okay."

Coop says he'll be okay, even if he clears waivers and the Saints
don't recall him. He says he's got another option. "I need to get in
touch with Jim (Vince) McMahon and the XFL so I can be the real shit
talker that I am."

He laughs. In his situation, there's nothing wrong with a little humor
and, there's a lot right with going home to be a husband and a daddy.

But what Coop doesn't realize is that it's already been decided that he's not coming back. Minutes after I leave Coop's company that afternoon, I learn that Bobby Setzer will be recalled to the practice squad. This information won't officially be released until two or three days from now, but my source is a reliable one. So when Haslett told Coop a few hours ago that the practice squad was a possibility for him, he already knew that it wasn't. In fact, last night, by the way Clancy talked and by his nervous body language, it seemed like it had already been decided *before* the game that Setzer was the man.

Setzer and not Cooper, go figure. The Saints the last 33 years, go figure that, too. But I don't want to get carried away. I don't want to psychoanalyze the Saints or their paranoid behavior about the media or anything else. The issue here is Setzer versus Cooper.

Really, Setzer could be one of our heroes. Coming out of Boise State in 1998, he wasn't drafted. He'd blown out his knee his senior year and wound up sitting out all of 1999. After originally signing a free agent contract with the Giants in January 2000, he was released a few weeks later and picked up by the Saints on March 23, 2000. Technically, he's an undrafted rookie, even though, unlike our original 10 heroes, he didn't sign his first NFL contract with the Saints.

Setzer has overcome injury and great odds to be where he is. He deserves the shot he's been given, and hopefully, it's the start of a great career. But as good as Setzer might become, he'll never be what Coop could be.

So why Setzer? The first person to ask would be the one who's watched Setzer and Coop the most. That's their position coach Sam Clancy. When he's questioned later this week, Clancy initially says all the right things. "It was like a flip of the coin. Cooper was showing signs early. Setzer was showing signs late."

When he's asked about the Miami game, and reminded that Coop made six tackles to Setzer's zero tackles, he says, "The ball was coming more to the right side, right where Cooper was. Everything was run away from Bobby." This is true in that Coop had more plays run toward his side. But on one of the plays run toward Setzer, Coop actually ran all the way from his side and made the tackle. The play is illustrative of Coop's athletic superiority.

The bottom line is Miami game or no Miami game, it is shocking that Clancy, who's been praising Coop since day one, is suddenly crawfishing. I ask him, "If it was you personally picking, who would you have selected?"

He responds, "Well, uh, you know, it's hard to say." He then gives a convoluted explanation, which ends with "so it's hard to say."

"If it was up to you personally, this thing, you probably couldn't give me an answer right now?"

"I really couldn't," he says.

He really couldn't because his answer is he would have kept Coop. That's the inference. He can't publicly say something that's contrary to what the boss has done.

So what does the boss say? At Haslett's press conference, a half hour later, I ask him, "Why'd you keep Setzer and not Cooper?"

"I think long-range he's gonna be a better football player," he says, adding, "I've never been asked a question about the practice squad before."

"Did Cooper have any negatives?"

"He was on the field when he wasn't supposed to be on the field, so we have 12 guys on the field. He doesn't line up right half the time."

"Did the mental mistakes kill him, would you say that?"

"I would say that."

So the head man has spoken. The statement, "He doesn't line up right half the time," sounds harsh and can't be true, which is perhaps why the media police created new words for Haslett, changing the sentence on the press conference's transcript to read, "He lined up in the wrong spot a few times." Whether the message is delivered through a doctored statement or through the real words, it was the mental mistakes that did Coop in, even though Clancy acknowledged that the mistakes were easy to make considering that Coop was the only rookie lineman being shuffled back and forth between tackle and end.

But on this Saturday afternoon, Coop doesn't know any of this. He doesn't know he won't be on the practice squad or that his ex-coach has said that he "doesn't line up right half the time." It's better that he not know these things, not now at least. It's better that he go home, hug his wife, kiss his baby girl, and give them all his attention. Soon, he will know what's happened and what's been said. And one day, he will get his chance to line up somewhere. And it will all be right. It will all be just perfect.

~

Sunday, August 27, 2000, Dawn

Right now, it all rides on Raynock. As the sun rises, Chase is the last man standing. If he makes it past 3 p.m. without hearing from the Saints, he's home free. If the Turk calls before that deadline, he's home to Montana.

Chase has been out of the loop lately. While his teammates were slugging it out against Miami, he was on a plane somewhere above the Arizona desert, flying east. He'd spent the afternoon in San Diego, where a noted orthopedist was examining his injured knee for a second opinion. The second opinion matched the original one—a subluxed patella resulting in a severe knee sprain.

Later this morning, Chase gets a call from Randy Mueller. This time, it's Mueller himself who bears the message. He tells Chase the team had planned to save a spot for him on the practice squad, but they can't. If they retain Chase and rehabilitate him in New Orleans, they'll have to burn up a roster spot. So instead, they offer him an injury settlement, which is the equivalent of two weeks' pay, and a plane ticket home to Billings. He takes it. Hopefully, he'll be able to bring his knee back up to playable strength in a few weeks. Unfortunately, by that time, his window in New Orleans may have closed. The offensive lineman the Saints sign to the practice squad in Chase's stead may be too good to let go.

That afternoon, when I speak to him, I ask him if he feels like he's been cut. "I don't know. It still hasn't really set in yet. I'm just sort of sitting around here right now, just packing up, trying to get out of here, you know."

With his plane not leaving until the morning, he's thinking about catching a movie tonight. A movie, that's what camp has been for him, a whole reel of ups and downs, zigs and zags. Perhaps, the curtain hasn't fallen yet. Perhaps, in a week or two, the ending will change.

At the moment, though, there's a bad echo around here. It's the sound a place makes when it's empty. And I can't help but feel the void myself.

~

Wednesday, August 30, 2000, 1:00 p.m.

Cheri Boudreaux has already heard the news. Her big blonde grizzly
has gone away. Her fantasies of Chase one day being her teddy bear
have turned into a cold reality. It's so tough, this unrequited love.
When she first learned that Chase had been cut, she shed enough tears
to flood all of Wal-Mart. Now here it is, a couple days later, and she
says, "Oh, I cried. I could still cry."

/ EIGHTEEN /

THE TUNNEL

SUNDAY, SEPTEMBER 3, 2000, 12:00 P.M.

Game day. There is only one way to get to there. It's the passage of all first passages. They've all imagined running through it. It might've been at Three Rivers or Mile High or Candlestick or the Coliseum. But most recently, it was this very funnel at this dome against these Detroit Lions. It was all about putting on the pads for real, feeling the uniform all snug and perfect, listening to the energy level rise, bursting out of darkness into a fantasia of light, feeling your bones rattle from the roar, hearing the announcer call out, "Ladies and Gentlemen, here come your New Orleans Saiiints!"

But they aren't your New Orleans Saints. Just the other day, they were. Now though, you're not anywhere on the roster, you can't be found on the practice squad. You can only watch what might have been on television.

You look at the screen, and you see a mostly veteran team. Mueller and Haslett have brought in veterans to start and veterans to back up. In a year or two, many of these older heads will be too old to be effective. While you admire Mueller and Haslett for wanting to win right now, you know that the plain reality is they shouldn't, not this season at least. You think they're intelligent and hungry, and you think they'll win one day. And that's just it, one day. You wonder why they don't see you as their future.

You're Jamal Brooks, and they cut you, then pick up a sixth-year linebacker called Donta' Jones, whom the Panthers have just released. They want to bring in an old guy to backup when you know you could do that, and all of your best days are ahead of you. You're D.J. Cooper, Robert Brannon, and Desmond Gibson, and you see how two of your former d-linemates, Robert Newkirk and Uhuru Hamiter, two Ditka guys, made the final 53, only to be cut a day later when the team claimed two guys who were cut from the Ravens. Their names are Marques Douglas and Martin Chase. Who the hell are they?

You're Pete Destefano, and the last two weeks don't make any sense. Cutting you was crazy enough, but then you see what happened to a good guy like your fellow safety, Gerald Vaughn, who's paid his dues with seven years in Canada. You see him make the final 53 and feel the NFL in his fingers, only to have his heart ripped out a day later when they cut him and pick up a drafted rookie corner who's been discarded by the Lions. For all you know, this Todd Franz might be good, but he hasn't spilled one drop of blood on Saints' soil, where you spent the better part of the last four months running yourself ragged and learning the system.

You, the released undrafted rookie, wonder why six players are on that sideline, be they on the roster or the practice squad, who didn't expel one drop of sweat in Thibodaux. That last minute turnover can't be good. And then you see why it isn't.

You watch the Lions' Desmond Howard grab a punt at the five-yard line and take it through a shuffled punt coverage team. You know that the guys in there aren't exactly who Coach Al Everest wanted in there. What is happening is not Al's fault. He's always said that many starters can't play special teams, and here he is having to play starters who have never played special teams. Here he is with a unit that didn't work together in training camp. That's the biggest objective of camp, to get overready for game one. And this unit isn't ready and can't be ready. That's obvious when Howard scoots and skips, making them look like amateurs. You see him score and get a feeling by the slow flow of this game that this score will be the difference.

As a matter of fact, these types of scores, long punt and kickoff returns, will kill the Saints during the early part of this season, causing Haslett to say that his team doesn't have enough young, energetic players to effectively play special teams.

It's not easy for you to hear this because you are that young, energetic player, and he could've kept you, but he didn't. Of course, he blames the lack of youth on the Saints' lack of quality draft picks the last few years, but you have an answer for that, too. Many of the best special-teamers in the modern game, Pro Bowl guys like Bill Bates, Bennie Thompson, and Larry Izzo, were all undrafted, or they were like Elbert Shelley, who as a 10th rounder wouldn't have been drafted today.

It's easy to know why you, the undrafted, do better than the instant tycoons. There's a reason why you are a hell-bent, scrappy, this-is-my-lane fighter. It's because you're fighting for food, not for Ferraris. It's because you'll do anything the coach asks you to do just to be on the field. The coach should know that he's not gonna convince a man with millions in mutual funds to throw his body into the wedge. The coach should know that if he's looking for a kamikaze cover-type, he should look at you.

You look at this game, this pitiful game. It's been tough for you to watch this, and it's been just plain tough ever since you got off that plane and had to face your family and friends and tell them that you failed. They give you their love and support and tell you they've still got your back. You realize how lucky you are to have them. But, by the same token, they have questions that you can't answer. You only know that you wake up every morning thinking for a second that you have to go to work, then realize you have nowhere to go. It's football season, and you don't have a football team. So you go to the gym, punish your body, and hope that your agent will call with good news. But so far, he hasn't.

Most of you remember that awful day sitting in Dr. Finney's office waiting with 11 others who'd been released just like you. You remember what second-year wide receiver P.J. Franklin said that day. This was a Ditka guy who would not be a Haslett guy, who said, "It wasn't competitive at all. It was all laid out from the beginning."

You listen to P.J., and you know he's telling the truth because you look at that starting lineup and at the backups, and everyone who's there seems like they were groomed to be there from the moment they signed a contract. There are no real surprises. There are no Ronney Jenkins-types, the San Diego Chargers' undrafted rookie kick returner, who blazed through coverage teams all through the preseason, and who, next week, will burst through the Saints' roster-shuffled kick coverage team for a 93-yard touchdown. In your opinion, there might have been some Ronney Jenkinses on the Saints, if only they'd let you compete with some of these guys who were penciled in from jumpstreet.

Of course, true or false, this sounds like sour apples. So you look at the TV set, and you try to find the positive, the inspiration. There's one in Sammy Knight, who's slaying the Lions with every draw of his sword. He steals a pass and scores the Saints' only touchdown. He plays the deep half, but he lives in the Lions' backfield. And he started out just like you, undrafted, as did Keith Mitchell, Phil Clarke, and Kevin Mathis, who are all first-teamers now, and who are spearheading a fine defensive effort.

So one day, you can be them. You may need to take Kurt Warner's path, tossing the Nerf in the supermarket aisles, then playing indoor ball, foreign ball, then the ball of all balls. Of course, many have gone that route but never made it back to the bigs even though they were good enough. They got too old or too labeled or too unlucky. So the odds are against you coming back to this league once you've left, but you're used to these odds. You've faced them ever since they didn't call your name on draft day.

When this game ends, it's easy to see that the Saints have lost, 10-14. It's not so easy to see that you have won. And, yes, you are victorious. You didn't win because the Saints lost. You won in the only contest that really counts—your life. A life lesson may the furthest thing from your mind right now, but that's what you've been given.

It's a gift because your life will be much better because you were rejected. That sounds nuts, but there is a chain of logic. It starts with Rick Venturi's saying. When he says, "Life is not fair in the National Football League," he should just say, "Life is not fair" because it's not. Of course, you already know this. Your personal lives have taught you as much. But, heck, when it came to football, it was always so easy. If you put in the work, you were going to succeed. If you were the best, you were going to play. It was always like that.

But nothing's like that, not always. The sooner you learn that, the better. You may be bitter toward the people that have taken this game away from you. You may even hate them for dashing you dreams. Remember, though, this isn't about them. This has never been their story. It's about you, and what you do with this.

It can become your rocket booster. The mere memory of how you feel now can fire you forward like nothing you've ever felt. It works as long as you don't accept this feeling, as long as you tell yourself you will never, if you can help it, feel this way again. What you've learned is sometimes you can't help it. Sometimes, you will be prejudiced, whether it's because you're undrafted or because you don't know the right people or because your pants are the wrong style. But prejudice can't and won't get in your way every time. Ultimately, only you will control your life.

You have a calling. It might be football. It might not be. But there is something out there for you. Your epilogue is what you will it to be. It may take six months. It may take 20 years. But in the end, it's all yours.

THE EPILOGUE
March 23, 2001

WHAT HAPPENED TO THE DREAMERS

They came in dreaming, eyes dancing with possibilities. They went out thinking, eyes hardened by reality. And they scattered. To the Pacific and Atlantic, to the Ozarks, Rockies, and Appalachians, to the Great Plains and Great North Woods, to college towns and cities, to wives and girlfriends, to mothers and fathers, to children, born and unborn. All of them looking for their next check, next chance, next chapter.

Chase Raynock was the last to go. He thought his time away would be temporary. He thought that once his knee healed, he would march back in to New Orleans. But the days of rehab and waiting turned into weeks, and the Saints never called.

Chase filled the void by teaching football. He volunteered to help the offensive line coach at the University of Montana. There, he broke down film, taught technique, told trench stories. He discovered that he loved it. It didn't matter that he wasn't getting paid for it. The experience was priceless.

Then in October, Chase received a call from an NFL team located just down the mountain range in Colorado. The Denver Broncos offered him a spot on their practice squad. Chase arrived in Denver on October 26 and was released on October 31. He said he never had much of a chance to make an impression. "They were shuffling guys in and out every week."

Chase returned to Missoula and sunk himself into coaching. He ended up going on an exhilarating ride with the Grizzlies all the way to a finish as the I-AA national runner-up.

While coaching quenched some of his thirst for the game, he still longed to play. He got his opportunity on December 29 when the Chicago Enforcers selected him with the first pick of the XFL supplemental draft. Although Chase downplayed the significance of being drafted and being chosen first overall, he must have felt vindicated. For someone who had once endured two days of draft dejection, he must have felt some sense of justice.

After the draft, Chase looked forward to being a part of the XFL's inaugural season. The league was promoted as an "xtreme" brand of football with rules that included no fair catches on punt returns and a lax roughing the passer penalty. One of the XFL's goals was to be more fan-friendly. To that end, its founder, World Wrestling Federation czar Vince McMahon, offered reasonable ticket prices and lots of romp and pomp at the games. Notable sideshows would include troupes of belly-baring, flirtatious cheerleaders, live sideline interviews of players, and offbeat, WWF-style color commentary. In a single game, the frenzied television viewer would be stirred by violence, gripped by drama, teased with sexuality, and tickled with comedy.

Additionally, the viewer would be treated to angles unexplored in an NFL broadcast. The cameras of league partner NBC, as well as the ones for UPN and TNN, were to follow the players into the locker room, where the TV audience would hear the coach's hardy pregame pep talk and bleep-ridden, halftime tongue-lashing. Also, intergalactic storm-trooper-like cameramen wearing protective equipment would actually shoot video within the field of play, aiming into the huddle, broadcasting the quarterback's every bark.

This promising new XFL world was what awaited Chase Raynock at Enforcers' training camp in Orlando in January. But what he found was "pretty much a disaster." He spent a week in what he classified as a chaotic Enforcers' camp. "In my opinion, it was just a terrible, terrible organization to play under and to be in, and I wanted nothing to do with it. I mean, it was terrible. Coaching-wise, I didn't think it was up to professional standards. I didn't even think it was up to high school standards.

"The whole time I was there, people were saying, 'The coaches don't know what they're doing. I'm gonna do my own thing when we get out on the field.' I told them I was not going to play for them, and I left camp. I said, 'Trade me or release me, but I'm not going to play for you guys.'" (Editor's Note: The Enforcers started the season 1-5, but won their next four games to finish 5-5 and earn a berth in the playoffs, where they lost in the first round.)

After returning to Montana, Chase was home for a week when he learned that he'd been traded to the New York/New Jersey Hitmen. He then flew back down to Orlando for the Hitmen's camp. After his arrival, he found out that the league was debating whether his trade was legal because, prior to the transaction, the Enforcers had placed Chase on the reserve/left camp list, which apparently meant that he was not allowed to play in the XFL that season.

So Chase waited in street clothes at the Hitmen's camp while the league deliberated over his status. "I never even practiced with them. I just stood around for five days waiting for the league to rule."

When the XFL finally nullified the trade, Chase traveled back to Montana. Then his wave ride crested again when midway through the season, Birmingham Bolts' coach Gerry DiNardo called and asked Chase if he'd like to come to Birmingham. Chase told him, "I'd love to." The Bolts then made a league-approved trade for Chase, and a few days later, Chase, in his very first game in a Bolts' uniform, actually started at left tackle against the Los Angeles Xtreme.

As for his Bolts' experience, he said during his second week in Birmingham, "I like the whole organization. I like the staff here. I like everything about this place."

And the cheerleaders? "Aww, that's great stuff. It's great stuff. It's hard to concentrate on the game sometimes looking over there. You get these girls pretty much doing a strip show on the side there."

After the XFL season's conclusion, Chase said he hopes to sign with an NFL team, as does his old roommate and current XFLer, Pete Destefano. While Pete said he is enjoying his role as a starting safety for the San Francisco Demons, he has had to fight a few mental devils since his days of combat in the hellish Saints' camp heat.

He wrote in a November 15, 2000 E-mail, "I think for me, it is harder now because I know I can do other things with my life. I have graduated from a wonderful university, which carries a lot of clout in the business world. However, I love football and know that I will eventually get my act together because I love to play the game."

Pete pined for the game so much that after only one week on the job as a technical recruiter in Silicon Valley, he left the position to concentrate on preparing for the XFL. During those preparations, while participating in a coverage drill in a predraft workout for the Demons, he received a scare when he sustained a spiral fracture down his left index finger. Fortunately, surgery was unnecessary, and the injury would heal in time for training camp. But unfortunately, his XFL contract created problems for San Francisco's NFL team when the 49ers approached Pete in December. Because Pete had signed with the Demons before the 49ers contacted him, the 49ers decided to back away from their initial invitation to him to join their practice squad. Pete would have relished spending the season's last two weeks with his childhood dream team, but it was not to be.

Pete's football adventure kept rolling at Demons' training camp in Las Vegas. He said the camp was a "rude awakening," differing from Saints' camp "in every way possible."

"We had to get dressed on the field. We didn't have a locker room," said Pete. "If anything could go wrong, it happened. Not enough shoulder pads for guys. Receivers wearing linemen shoulder pads. Quarterbacks trying to throw in linebacker pads. It was pretty much a joke."

The practice field was far from the soft fairways of the NFL. "It was just real, real hard. It was like concrete," he said. While the weather in cool Nevada was generally more pleasant than in steamy Louisiana, Pete noted, "One week, it was absolutely freezing. It went from being nice to being freezing." As for the food, he said it wasn't bad, but it was "the same food over and over again for a month. That gets kind of old."

Overall, his feelings about the XFL during camp were "not very good." "You know, they tried to make everything happen so fast. I think they overlooked a lot of things."

Nonetheless, Pete liked his coaches and loved taking part in a come-from-behind, last-second victory over the Los Angeles Xtreme before a packed Pac Bell Park on opening day. During halftime in the locker room, the UPN camera repeatedly focused on Pete's steely mug. His friends later ribbed him about the national TV face time.

Despite missing some game action after experiencing successive concussions, Pete has played well and said about the XFL experience, "It's been a good one, actually." He then added jokingly, "Our checks haven't been bouncing. So that's always a good sign."

~

Pete's current brother in the XFL, D.J. Cooper, had been itching to play in the new league since he left New Orleans. So when the Memphis Maniax selected him with the 46th overall pick of the draft, he said, "It felt good. It felt like somebody actually liked me, like I'm a La'Roi Glover for somebody."

But before he played one snap for the Maniax, an NFL team called him at his Fayetteville, Arkansas home. The Chicago Bears invited him to join their practice squad, and he signed with them on December 8. "They hit Christmas right on time," said Coop.

When Chicago also agreed to let him play in the XFL after the NFL season concluded, Coop couldn't believe his coup. "I've been a Walter Payton fan forever," he said of the former Bear. "Just to be up there in Soldier Field was great for me. If you can come to my house from '82 to '92, all you would see was Bears stuff all over my room. That was a good thing for me, too, that I got to even go up there and be thought of as a part of the team."

Coop said he spent a productive three weeks in Chicago. "I felt a little bit more comfortable (than when in Saints' camp). I didn't feel like I was getting pointed at all the time. You know, the d-line coach, he had pull. You can tell that if he said something to the head coach or something like that, it could probably go somewhere. And he really liked me. He thought I had all the potential in the world, and he treated me like I had all the potential in the world. He didn't make me feel like I was just a body.

"I always felt like a body down there (in Saints' camp). You know, 'cause they would say one thing, then it would change. Then I'll have a pretty decent game, but you know I'll make mental errors. But I thought they would expect mental errors from rookies. Then I have tackles in each preseason game, and Bobby Setzer didn't have any, really, in none of the games, and he gets picked up. (Note: Setzer finished with two tackles. Coop led all Saints' rookie defenders with nine tackles.) Like I said, it's politics, and I'm not one for politics."

In the XFL, Coop traded politics for pizzazz and pure football. He said although training camp in Las Vegas was a little disorganized, it didn't bother him. "This is just the first year. You really can't expect too much out of it for the first year."

He said that in Vegas, some of his teammates started to get grumpy when their paychecks didn't arrive when they expected. "You know you got a lot of attitudes and this and that because you not getting paid and all this and that. You know I was just down there loving it. Like I said, I'm a big WWF fan and that was all I wanted to do was just come to the XFL. And I really wasn't caring about the money. I was just down there..." He cackled. "Killing!"

One of the highlights of camp for Coop was meeting Vince McMahon. "He's just like how he talk on TV, just more mellow." The definite lowlight was sustaining a torn left posterior cruciate ligament (PCL) in his left knee. Doctors, however, told him that surgery wouldn't be necessary.

While the injury caused Coop to miss the season's first four games, when he returned to action he was able to play effectively at defensive end. He said he was only about 80%, but his recovery has progressed steadily.

He said he's confident that his injury will resolve in time for him to get another shot with the Bears or another NFL team. But he said in the meantime, he's having a ball battling in the league of xtremes. "(The XFL games) are wild. The fans are wild. You got the guns going off, the firecrackers going off. You got the women in the background shaking it up. You got the big Jumbotron screen that you get to see everything that's going on. It's pretty nice."

Coop's old roommate, Desmond Gibson, applied for the XFL but wasn't drafted by the league. Giving up on football, though, wasn't an option for him. "There's so much more that I have to offer that wasn't even seen," he said, noting that he only played two quarters in the first Saints' preseason game and didn't play at all in the next two games.

So in the fall, as Desmond waited for another chance to play, he labored through each weekday from 9 to 5 doing pharmaceutical research for a firm in downtown Pittsburgh. When asked what company he worked for, he became the private son of preachers and responded, "Well, I really don't want to put that in there." He added, "It was pretty much just a job to pass the time."

Desmond also spent his days playing the drums, hanging out at the church and dealing with being a football-less man in a place where he was once a football idol. "It was kind of rough a little bit in the beginning, especially watching a lot of my buddies play and things like that. But then it kind of started feeling like a redshirt year since I never redshirted. It just gave me a lot of time to work on my game and just work out and stuff like that."

In February, Desmond learned that all of his self-imposed workouts would be in preparation for another opportunity, this one with the Winnipeg Blue Bombers of the CFL. He said that he's excited about playing in an established, albeit frozen, league, but also added, "Be looking for me in the NFL pretty soon."

Coincidentally, joining Desmond on the Blue Bombers this summer will be his former Saints' teammate and fellow Pennsylvania native, Terrence Miles. Terrence said he refused to dwell on the Saints cutting him on his birthday on just the third morning of camp. "I really haven't thought about it too much," he said. "After it actually happened, I kind of dealt with it my own little way. And I put it behind me, put it in the past."

Despite letting bygones be bygones, Terrence still felt a void. "It's not a good feeling. I mean returning back to school and everything, watching my school play. You want to be out there. You want to be playing, even if it's not actually playing for the school or the NFL. You want to be playing football."

While the Saints delayed his NFL aspirations, they made it possible for him to fulfill another dream. Because Terrence was cut early, he had time to register for 15 hours of classes towards his Kutztown University degree in general studies with a dual minor in criminal justice and social work.

On December 16, Terrence put on a uniform more honorable than an NFL jersey. He then took steps never taken by anyone in his family. The stage on which he traversed might as well have been a great stadium. The diploma in his hand was a symbol of hard work and history.

Educated and graduated, Terrence deservedly and humbly walked tall.

~

Moving down the Atlantic seaboard, in Virginia, Shayne Graham was trying to become the first person in his family to kick a football for a living. He received his first chance a few games into the NFL season when the Jacksonville Jaguars' kicker, Mike Hollis, injured his back. The Jaguars brought in Shayne and two other kickers for a workout. Shayne felt at ease at the Jaguars' practice field, having kicked there with the Saints and as a sophomore at Virginia Tech during Gator Bowl week. During the tryout, Shayne believed that he outkicked his competitors, including Chris Boniol, formerly of Dallas, Philadelphia, and Chicago. The Jaguars, however, elected to use their kickoff specialist, Steve Lindsey, to kick field goals until Hollis returned from the injury.

Then, as the weeks passed, and kickers were being shuffled on and off rosters throughout the NFL, Shayne felt that he should've been receiving more inquiries. Around midseason he decided to fire his agent, who Shayne believed was unfairly favoring another kicker client. "I just felt that he had let a few things fall through the cracks. I'm not going to blame it on him. I just know I've done better since him."

Unfortunately, Shayne wouldn't begin to do better until the NFL season ended. After the season, he moved from Blacksburg, Virginia to the Virginia suburbs of Washington, D.C., and moved into the family home of his kicking coach, Fred Pinciaro. His schedule has since gone into warp speed.

In addition to taking nine hours of classes via the Internet, Shayne is working three jobs, practicing his kicking, and putting himself through the most strenuous fitness regimen of his life. In the mornings and afternoons, he substitute teaches at local high schools. In the evenings, he kicks, then conditions at a Gold's Gym franchise, where he also works part-time. On weekends, he's an instructor at Fourth Down Sports, a traveling kicking clinic.

Professionally, since signing on with a new agent, Shayne notched a workout with the Birmingham Bolts, but XFL kicking specialists must kick and punt, and Shayne's punting wasn't consistent enough to earn a contract. He also worked out for the Carolina Cobras of the

Arena League, who invited him to their training camp.

As for the Saints, Shayne has been keeping close tabs on their topsy-turvy kicking situation. "I don't know what's going on down in New Orleans," he said. In December, Saints' kicker Doug Brien was in a bit of a slump, and the team brought in five kickers for workouts. Shayne was surprised that he wasn't one of them. "It kind of gave me a shot to the ego, I guess. I don't know. I would've expected they would've called me, but they went to guys who were veterans." The Saints ultimately stuck with Brien, who nailed his last 11 field goals of the season. Then on March 1, out of the blue, the Saints released Brien.

Well, on March 22, Shayne got some news that made the Saints' situation irrelevant. On the last day of a minicamp invite with the Seattle Seahawks, Shayne nailed all of his field goals. Even with his perfect performance, he walked into the locker room after practice still puzzled about his future. Then, from around the corner came the Seahawks' renowned special teams coordinator, Pete Rodriguez. Rodriguez had a contract in his hand.

As Shayne received and clutched the paper promise, all the months of rejection disappeared, all the weeks of nonstop work made sense. One of the league's best had just confirmed his confidence. Although Shayne had made moon shots at lesser leagues, he'd instead hit the sun by getting a chance to play for a special teams guru and a Super Bowl-winner in head coach Mike Holmgren.

While Shayne still must beat out incumbent Rian Lindell to make the Seattle squad, he said he's never felt better about his chances.

An NFL chance arose for defensive tackle Robert Brannon just a few weeks after leaving Saints' camp. The New York Jets, impressed with Robert's brief performance against them in preseason, brought him in for a tryout. But the Jets didn't offer him a contract; and the next development in Robert's life would be much more monumental.

On October 10, 2000, in Big Bear, California, Robert's fiancée Stacy gave birth to a nine-pound girl named Kamryn. Robert's mother Darlene said of her son's first child, "She looks just like Robert."

By that point, Robert, propelled by the need for diapers and formula, had already begun working 12-hour days at the Chevron refinery in El Segundo. His rotation was roughly 30 days on, 14 off. His first assignment was the scaffolding crew, helping to assemble the scaffolding and to carry materials to people working on the towers. He sometimes worked 100-plus feet from the ground. While standing at those dizzying heights, Robert often asked himself what he was doing up there when he should have been down in the grass chasing quarterbacks. On the scaffolding, his 320-pound body was secured with a safety harness, but he said, "I don't know if that thing would have worked with me."

"It wasn't paying enough for me, man, to go up that high and build them scaffolds and haul them materials. Man, that's too much." He requested and received a transfer to another crew. "I went to fire watch, where all you do is sit there and look at people weld and everything."

As Robert's days at the refinery began to drag and blur he started to pursue a shot at the XFL. Then just before Christmas, he received a nice surprise. "I wasn't even expecting a call from the NFL people really." The Broncos invited him to Denver for a look-see on December 26. After Broncos officials watched Robert perform his drills, they handed him a contract. "It was my Christmas present," he said. At that moment, with Robert's head wafting among the aspen trees and the clean Colorado clouds, the smoke and smog of his L.A. refinery had never seemed so distant.

~

Unlike Robert Brannon, Amp Campbell is no longer playing the game. Just two and a half weeks after the Saints sent him back to East Lansing, Michigan, Amp received a job offer from Michigan State. Next thing Amp knew, he had gone from playing football to counseling football players as the Spartans' first-ever, "Coordinator of Football Player Development."

While Amp said he misses playing the sport, he feels at home in his new career. And as for his former occupation, he said although he has no hard feelings toward the Saints, he thinks they "mistreated" him by releasing him on just the second day of camp and by sending him packing without giving him an explanation as to why he was cut.

Nevertheless, he said he has moved on. "As soon as I got to East Lansing, I think it was behind me. I wasn't upset. I wasn't as angry as I thought I would be. I mean I think it was a sign of relief," he said. "You just feel as a person when you was there that you wasn't really wanted, you know. You only getting one rep in certain practices, and then you might only get three reps (in another practice). I could've been sitting at home doing the same thing that I was doing there."

Amp said after he returned home, he decided that the stigma of his neck injury would prevent him from getting an unbiased look from another NFL club. "It wasn't worth leaving my family here and going out and trying to play football again. Really, I did what I wanted to do, which was come back and play my last year at Michigan State, and if the NFL was something that I could have did, then I would have loved to have done it, but I just sat down and thought about some things after I got released, and I thought, you know, there's life after football, and I didn't need it. And I wasn't given a fair opportunity when I was there, and after that, I just said I'm going to go ahead and go out in the working world."

Amp eventually wants to get into coaching, but for now, he said he's content. "I'm still around football," he said. "I enjoy getting up every morning and coming to work."

While Amp has put his playing days behind him, his fellow former Saints' cornerback, Carlos Posey, said he's on track to play in 2001. After being released by the Saints *before* training camp, Posey spent the fall doing odd jobs in his native Baton Rouge. Since then, he has worked out for the NFC Champion New York Giants, and he has received an offer from the CFL's Montreal Alouettes. He said he'd sign with the Alouettes if an NFL option didn't materialize.

~

While the NFL season was in full swing, Jamal Brooks spent his days "working full-time and training full-time" while residing with his mother in suburban Atlanta, Georgia. During weekday mornings, he put himself through a tortuous conditioning program. Then, at 2 p.m., he clocked in at a Copy Club in Norcross, where he did computer graphics work until 11 p.m. He also found time for a new girlfriend, DeAnne Davis, a former All-American track star at North Carolina, who said she plans to train for the 2004 Olympics in the triple jump.

By January, Davis' boyfriend was jumping to put on the pads and take the field. Jamal had grown antsy watching his fellow ex-Saints' linebackers, Joe Tuipala and Ron Merkerson, tear up the XFL. "I'm saying, 'Man, they out there balling. If they out there balling, I know I could be doing my thing.'"

Jamal thought for sure he would be balling with the Saints. The team had kept in contact with him since he left camp. On several occasions, including during Jamal's exit interview, the Saints had indicated that they'd eventually sign him to a contract and allocate him to NFL Europe. In fact, new linebacker coach Winston Moss (the old linebacker coach, John Bunting, is now the head coach at the University of North Carolina) called Jamal the day he got the job and told him that he was his "number one guy" to allocate.

In the end, though, the Saints didn't make an offer. When Jamal realized that it wasn't going to happen, he was "disappointed" and a little "numb." But he said, "I know they (the Saints) didn't allocate no linebackers so that softened the blow a little bit." The impact was also reduced by the fact that Jamal had worked out on February 7 for the Tampa Bay Buccaneers and had been receiving inquiries from the NFL expansion Houston Texans, who begin play in 2002. Things continued to get better when the Scottish Claymores selected Jamal with the 14th pick of the NFL Europe free agent draft, making him the first linebacker taken.

Jamal said he believes a solid performance in the NFLEL will garner him another big league shot, probably with Tampa Bay, whose representatives have continued to call him every week. "If I do what I got to do, I'm 95% sure I'll be with the Buccaneers next year," he said. "If I don't go to the Saints, it's gonna be more their loss than my loss."

For now, however, Jamal said his focus is solely on Claymores' training camp and the ensuing season abroad. It will be his first time in Europe. As a temporary resident of Glasgow, will Jamal start wearing kilts and take up the bagpipes? "Naa, naa," he said. "I'm actually trying to learn to become a better player. You know, I'm a linebacker first. And the first thing with a linebacker is hitting somebody. And I ain't hit somebody in a while."

Joining Jamal Brooks in Europe will be one of his ex-partners in black and gold, punter Bill LaFleur. Bill is coming off a frigid fall and winter in Nebraska, where he spent his days honing his skills and working at his shooting and hunting business. He's now happy to be in balmy Tampa, the site of the NFLEL training camp. He's also ready to use his classroom Spanish as the new gringo punter for the Barcelona Dragons. "I think it'll be fun. I think it'll be an interesting experience," he said. "It's a chance to play football and do it in another culture."

Bill was allocated to the league by a familiar NFL team. He happens to be the only one of our heroes currently under contract with the New Orleans Saints.

To make the 2001 New Orleans squad, Bill will still have to beat out veteran Toby Gowin again. But he figures that with a full European season, he'll have the film necessary to attract another NFL team if he fails to stick with the Saints.

~

What Happened to the Team without Our Heroes

In the beginning, it was the September Saints, marching in, moving back, making a mockery. They were 1-3, and the score was the same. For all the new era optimism, they still couldn't throw the football and still couldn't cover a kickoff or a punt.

So Randy Mueller started looking for cover guys and began working over the bottom of the roster, making transactions as frequently as an old lady pulling a slot machine. Cutting and signing, and for why and for whom when Pete Destefano and Jamal Brooks could've covered up those kicks like hammering human gloves.

But then, woom, Mueller made a few moves and in came Fred McAfee and Corey Terry, and they were covering. And woosh, Jim Haslett and his staff made a few adjustments and up stepped Jeff Blake, and they were throwing. And vroom, Ricky Williams was still running. And whap, the offensive line was still blasting big tunnels. And crunch, the defense was still crushing.

Then it was the October Saints, marching in, moving up, making marvelous history. The wins began to mount. Six in a row, 7 and 3 and counting. Wasn't any stopping 'em until...

The last game, when Ricky went down with a broken ankle, and the next game, when Blake fell out with a fractured foot.

In walked Aaron Brooks, QB. He was the same quiet, skinny Brooks who was throwing wobbly balls in his first few days in

Thibodaux. Suddenly, Brooks was staring down St. Louis, the defending Super Bowl champs. But Brooks wasn't the one rattled. He was the one rattling and rolling through the Rams, beating 'em 31-24.

Then over the next three games, the Saints went 2-1 and secured, somehow, a playoff berth and, some way, the NFC Western Division Championship.

In the playoffs, the Saints and Rams met for a third time in New Orleans for the wild-card game. And this time, a voodoo priestess was out there before kickoff, conjuring up something to lift a 34-year-old curse. But this time, Haslett's offensive hand was loaded with backups at all six skill positions. Yet this time, the Rams were in ruin, 28-31. And for the first time ever, the Saints had scored a playoff victory.

In the crowd, the Who Dats were hooting, hugging, and second-lining. Out in TV land, the honorary Who Dats, the men who once wore the *fleur-de-lis*, were grinning and waving imaginary pennants.

"I was just cheering for 'em," said Coop. "My wife hated me cheering for 'em, too. I was like, 'Hey, I know those people. I know all them. I done sweated with them dudes. So I wanted them to have the biggest success in the world.'"

"Man, I was happy for 'em to tell you the honest truth," said Pete.

"I could feel the excitement," said Desmond. "It was like an 'I wish I could've been there' type of excitement. Then seeing on the sideline, seeing some of the guys that you were out in that 125° weather with, I mean I wanted them to win."

One week after the first playoff victory, the Saints swept upriver to Minneapolis. While the Vikings quickly buried them in an overwhelming aerial attack, the Saints' season, as a whole, was a surprising smash. Eleven and seven overall, Haslett named NFL Coach of the Year, and Mueller, NFL Executive of the Year. Sure, the Saints only beat one team with a winning record (and sure, they cut our heroes). But still, even Haslett admitted to this writer during camp, "I know it's not going to happen overnight. It's gonna take some time."

Do four games count as "some time?" While Mueller/Haslett's instant prosperity may have shocked the football universe, most of the Dreamers seem to have expected it. "I wasn't surprised," said Amp. "I knew that the way that Coach Zook was on defense, and how hard they worked, that they was going to be good."

"Everyone that I met there," said Chase, "they knew what they wanted, and they did it."

"Just having the chance to be inside," said Desmond, "and seeing the caliber of players that the Saints had, I couldn't imagine there being too many players in the world that much better."

Arguably, the Dreamers helped make them better. They helped shape that team during the Thibodaux toil. Some of the team's success had to come from Chase busting it against La'Roi Glover and Joe Johnson, from Desmond, Coop, and Robert leaning hard on Willie Roaf, from Pete sticking it to Joe Horn, and from Jamal spreading the juice to Keith Mitchell and Mark Fields. Our heroes made these great players greater and pushed all six of them to the Pro Bowl.

Some of the Dreamers should have been around to live the dream. But in hindsight, it's hard to criticize Mueller, Haslett, and company. All things considered, they were magical.

~

For our Dreamers, the stakes this summer will be the same as last year. Whether they'll be playing in the NFL, in another league or in another game of life altogether, they'll still be competing. But it's hard to believe that of the original 10 undrafted rookies that arrived in Thibodaux last July, more of them are scheduled to play for the Winnipeg Blue Bombers than for the Saints.

One of the future Blue Bombers, Desmond Gibson, said about his stint in the big league, "It was something that a lot of people dream of doing and seeing, but I mean it just gives you more of a reality-based check on what the life is of the professional athlete, and how it could be here today and gone tomorrow. And you really have to take the time to get a lot of other things established because it's just so quick, you know, in and out."

As of now, while almost all of our Dreamers are out of New Orleans, they're very much still in the hunt, still in search of their destiny. It's just as Jamal Brooks put it the last time we spoke. Before he hung up the phone, he said, "Don't end it too soon. Just leave it as to be continued."

All right, Jamal. To be continued...

To Susie

~

ACKNOWLEDGMENTS

I GREW UP WITH FARAWAY DREAMS. I thought that if something important were going to happen to me, it would unfortunately have to take place a long way from Thibodaux, Louisiana. I never imagined that my hometown would give me my start in the book world—even after I moved back here in 1999. So first, I thank the people of Thibodaux for leading the Saints here, which led me to write a book proposal, which led Sleeping Bear Press to take a chance on a rookie not yet drafted by the publishing industry. At Sleeping Bear, there are many people to acknowledge, including but not limited to Brian Lewis, visionary publisher, Vivian Collier, copyeditor extraordinaire, Lynne Johnson and her artful production team, including Felicia Macheske, Ritu Joshi, and Carolyn Flintoft, and Adam Rifenberick, shrewd editor, motivational coach and tireless town crier. Adam deserves a special credit. Had it not been for him, I wouldn't be writing these words, and this story would have never landed on a bookshelf.

Several people helped this book come together. My former secretary, Tracy Richardson, helped keep the paperwork organized. She also kept watch back at the office while I was out under the sun, chasing dreams. Ben Fairchild assisted with research. My media colleagues provided me with fellowship, favors, and facts. My current secretary, Simone Chauvin, was a key aid during the editing and publicity process. Webmaster Mike Pasieka masterfully constructed my Web site, www.woodyfalgoux.com. Photographers Kim Smith and

Doug Keese provided potential photos for the book and the site. And all people interviewed herein should be acknowledged for their contributions. Lastly, Dr. Barry Landry is responsible for making a great save as this story came to a conclusion.

Because this is my first published book, I'd also like to mention the people who helped my writing creep towards publication. Sylvia Thigpen Zeringue was the first teacher who suggested to me that I might do something useful in this area, and I will always be grateful for her early encouragement. I wish there was enough space to list all my mentors at St. Genevieve School, E.D. White Catholic High School, the University of Missouri and LSU Law School. I also wish it was possible to name all of my fellow writers who have patiently read my work over the years. Their red ink has been invaluable.

My greatest guidance comes from my family. Merely thanking my wife Susie isn't good enough. Only worship and countless paybacks will suffice. She put up with a lot during the 10 weeks it took to cover this story and blitz through the writing of it to make the first draft deadline. She and my young daughter Gracie kept me going, even though Gracie's inspiration appeared mostly through smiles and burps. My in-laws, the Gauthiers, have been helpful in several, countless ways. My sisters, Angelle and Nicole, have not only been supportive siblings but brutal editors (Nicole has been especially ferocious). Then there're my parents, who can be acknowledged more easily than they can be thanked. Daddy, thanks for setting the example, and Momma, thanks for your undying faith.

Great faith is what I have in our ten heroes. Their lives should be good ones. They were certainly good to me during this project. They didn't have to give me time when they had little time to give. I apologize to them for any undue harassment. But I won't apologize for rooting for them. I can't wait to see what happens next.